ELSTON HOWARD • JORGE POSADO ... ... G •

MBLISS • TINO MARTINEZ • TONY LAZZERI • JOE

H • JERRY COLEMAN • GIL MCDOUGALD • DEREK

TTI • MARK KOENIG • GRAIG NETTLES • RED ROLFE

WINFIELD • BOB MEUSEL • CHARLIE KELLER • ROY

GGIO • MICKEY MANTLE • BERNIE WILLIAMS • EARLE

ACKSON • ROGER MARIS • PAUL O'NEILL • TOMMY

ASCHI • MEL STOTTLEMYRE • WAITE HOYT • LEFTY

PAT • ANDY PETTITTE • WHITEY FORD • MARIANO

ETTI • JOE PAGE • CASEY STENGEL • JOE MCCARTHY

HUGGINS • YOGI BERRA • BILL DICKEY • THURMAN

U GEHRIG • DON MATTINGLY • MOOSE SKOWRON •

RI • JOE GORDON • BOBBY RICHARDSON • WILLIE

REK JETER • PHIL RIZZUTO • TONY KUBEK • FRANK

OLFE • CLETE BOYER • WADE BOGGS • JOE DUGAN •

OY WHITE • HANK BAUER • GENE WOODLING • JOE

EARLE COMBS • MICKEY RIVERS • BABE RUTH

MMY HENRICH • RED RUFFING • ALLIE REYNOLDS •

TY GOMEZ • RON GUIDRY • HERB PENNOCK • YOGI

# FEW AND CHOSEN

# FEW AND CHOSEN

*Defining Yankee Greatness Across the Eras*

# Whitey Ford

## with Phil Pepe

Foreword by Yogi Berra

## TRIUMPH
B O O K S

CHICAGO

Library of Congress Cataloging-in-Publication Data

Ford, Whitey, 1928–
    Few and chosen : defining Yankee greatness across the eras / Whitey Ford with Phil Pepe.
      p.   cm.
    Includes index.
    ISBN 1-57243-418-X (hardcover)
    1. New York Yankees (Baseball team)   2. Baseball players—United States—Biography.   I. Pepe, Phil.   II. Title.

GV875.N4 F65   2001
796.357′64′097471—dc21                2001033606

This book is available in quantity at special discounts for your group or organization. For further information, contact:

**Triumph Books**
601 South LaSalle Street
Suite 500
Chicago, Illinois 60605
(312) 939-3330
Fax (312) 663-3557

Printed in the United States of America

ISBN 1-57243-418-X

*To Joan, Sally Ann, Eddie, and Tommy*

# Contents

# Foreword

I HAVE HAD MANY GREAT HONORS IN MY LIFE, which I am still living now, but none greater than knowing that my friend and my old battery mate, Whitey Ford, has picked me as the No. 1 catcher in Yankees history.

I always said Whitey was the smartest pitcher I ever caught. And the best.

I thought so much of Whitey's knowledge of pitching that, when the Yankees named me to manage the team after Ralph Houk moved up to general manager in 1964, I asked Whitey to be my pitching coach—even though he was still an active player at the time. I figured Whitey was one guy who could pitch and coach at the same time.

To me, choosing Whitey to be my pitching coach was a no-brainer. We had been together for so many years. I was his catcher for probably 95 percent of his starts in his 12 seasons with the Yankees and I respected him as a winner, a thinking man's pitcher, and as a competitor. I figured he was the right guy to teach our young pitchers his experiences.

I have known Whitey longer than just about anybody alive. I first met him in 1946. It was late in the season and the Yankees had just brought me up from Newark. Whitey had just been signed by the Yankees and he had come to Yankee Stadium to sign his contract. They took him through the clubhouse to meet the guys and somebody introduced him to me as "Eddie Ford." And they introduced me to him as "Larry Berra."

The next time I saw him was during the 1950 season, when the Yankees brought him up from Kansas City. He won nine games for us and lost only one, and helped us win the pennant. I knew right away that he was going to be a special pitcher. And he was. The best.

I even attended Whitey and Joan's wedding in April of 1951. I wasn't personally invited to the wedding—we weren't that close back then—but the whole team went by bus to his wedding reception in Queens after we had played an exhibition game against the Brooklyn Dodgers.

In my 17 years with the Yankees, we won 14 pennants and 10 World Series. I always thought we should have won the 1960 World Series and made it 11. That was the year Casey Stengel chose to hold Whitey out of the first game, so he pitched only twice against the Pittsburgh Pirates. He shut them out both times. I'm sure if he had pitched against them three times, he would have won all three games and we would have been world champions again.

We won the pennant in 1964, my first year as manager, and again I thought we should have beat the Cardinals in the World Series. Whitey started the first game and got knocked out in the sixth inning. When he tried to pitch, he couldn't even reach home plate. It turned out he had some kind of circulation problem and he couldn't pitch again for the rest of the Series. We lost to the Cardinals in seven games, but I'm sure if Whitey had been healthy and could have started two more times, we would have beaten the Cardinals and I would not have been fired. I might still be managing the Yankees today.

I never expected to be fired after we won the pennant. In fact, on the plane ride home from St. Louis, I talked to Whitey and asked him to come back the next year as my pitching coach. And he agreed. The next day, I was told I was fired.

It's funny how things turn out. All these years later, more than 50 years, Whitey is still one of my best friends. He made the Hall of Fame and I made the Hall of Fame. He had his number retired by the Yankees and I had my number retired by the Yankees. I wrote a book and he has written a book, and he named me the No. 1 catcher in Yankees history.

All I can say is, thank you, Whitey, for making this necessary.

—YOGI BERRA
April 2001

# Preface

THE SUCCESS OF THE NEW YORK YANKEES is unmatched in the annals of sport in this country. They are the most famous, most celebrated, most renowned team in baseball or, for that matter, in any sport.

From their nomadic beginning in 1903—when the Baltimore Orioles were purchased for $18,000 by Frank Farrell, a gambling entrepreneur, and Bill Devery, a former New York City chief of police, and moved to New York—through the year 2000, the Yankees (known for the first 10 years of their existence as the New York Highlanders), won 37 American League pennants and 26 World Series championships. No other team even comes close.

The Athletics, for example, have won fourteen pennants in two cities (eight in Philadelphia, six in Oakland), and nine World Series (five in Philadelphia, four in Oakland). The Boston Red Sox and Detroit Tigers have each won nine American League pennants. The Red Sox won the World Series five times, the Tigers four.

In the National League, the Dodgers have won eighteen pennants in two cities (Brooklyn and Los Angeles), and six World Series. The St. Louis Cardinals, with fifteen National League pennants, have won nine World Series.

But the Yankees stand head and shoulders above the rest. In their 98 years, the Yankees have won 38 percent of the American League pennants and 27 percent of baseball's World Series.

These numbers are even more staggering if you consider that the Yankees did not win their first pennant until 1921. So, in an 80-year period, the

Yankees have won 46 percent of the American League pennants and 32 percent of the World Series.

To achieve such success the Yankees obviously had to have great players. They have had some of the greatest ever to play the game, at all positions. Thirty-three Yankees players and four managers are in the Baseball Hall of Fame.

With so much talent to choose from, it is obviously no easy task to select the all-time Yankees team—the top five players at each position and the top five managers in Yankees history. But there is no one as uniquely qualified to attempt such a challenge as Edward "Whitey" Ford.

Elected to the Hall of Fame himself in 1974, Ford was a teammate of six Hall of Famers and the coach of another. He was born and raised in New York, has lived in New York all his life, and saw his first Yankees game 62 years ago. For the past 50 years, he has been part of the Yankees family.

—PHIL PEPE
Englewood, New Jersey
May 2001

# Introduction

I WAS BORN IN NEW YORK, JUST A FEW MILES from Yankee Stadium. As a kid, I was a Yankees fan; I saw my first Yankees game in 1938, when I was nine.

As a Yankee for 16 seasons, I had the privilege of playing with six Hall of Famers—Joe DiMaggio, Phil Rizzuto, Yogi Berra, Mickey Mantle, Johnny Mize, and Enos Slaughter—and for one Hall of Fame manager, Casey Stengel. In my brief tenure as a pitching coach for the Yankees, I coached another Hall of Famer, Catfish Hunter.

I have lived all my life in New York and have remained close to the Yankees. I get to about 10 or 12 games a year, and I follow them on television. In the spring, I usually spend a few weeks in training camp, and I used to run a fantasy camp in Fort Lauderdale, where my instructors are all former Yankees.

I have kept up with the Yankees through the years. Still, I find that trying to pick an all-time Yankees team, the top five players at each position, is a huge task. There have been so many great players that I'm afraid I'm going to overlook someone—especially among those I never saw play.

Of course, there are some no-brainers. How could you leave out Babe Ruth, Lou Gehrig, Joe DiMaggio, or Mickey Mantle? You don't have to have seen them play to know that they belong on the list. With other players who were before my time, I have had to rely on their records and the things I've heard from those who saw them play.

I have tried to judge the players strictly on their years with the Yankees, not their entire careers. As a result, some players, such as Roger Clemens, Phil Niekro, Mize, and Slaughter, who certainly deserve recognition on any all-star team based on their outstanding careers, might not make it onto my all-time Yankees team because they weren't Yankees for long enough.

In any case, I want to emphasize that there's nothing official about these selections. They are merely my opinion.

—WHITEY FORD
Fort Lauderdale, Florida
May 2001

# FEW AND CHOSEN

# ONE

# Catcher

M Y ALL-TIME YANKEES TEAM STARTS behind the plate with the catchers. Why catchers? I'll answer that question by quoting my old manager, Casey Stengel.

After he was fired by the Yankees for failing to win the 1960 World Series (although we did outscore the Pittsburgh Pirates 55–27 in the seven games), Stengel sat out a year, and then, at the age of 72, was hired as the first manager of the New York Mets in 1962.

To stock that first Mets team, the National League had an expansion pool of players; with their first pick, the Mets selected veteran catcher Hobie Landrith off the San Francisco Giants roster.

When reporters asked him why the Mets made Landrith their first pick,
Stengel explained the selection as only he could: "Because you gotta have a catcher," he said. "If you don't have a catcher, you're liable to have a lot of passed balls."

So, I start my all-time Yankees team with the catchers. With this quintet of catchers, there won't be many passed balls.

1. YOGI BERRA

2. BILL DICKEY

3. THURMAN MUNSON

4. ELSTON HOWARD

5. JORGE POSADA

In a 51-year period, from 1929 through 1979, four men did the bulk of the catching for the Yankees in 43 seasons. They are (from left): Hall of Famers Bill Dickey and Yogi Berra, Elston Howard, and Thurman Munson.

I'm sure you've heard a lot through the years about the Yankees' legacy of great center fielders, from Earle Combs to Joe DiMaggio to Mickey Mantle, all the way to the incumbent, Bernie Williams. Although it has not been as well publicized, the same is true of Yankees catchers, from Wally Schang, who was the catcher for those great Yankees teams in the early twenties, to Bill Dickey to **Yogi Berra** to Elston Howard to Thurman Munson.

For 33 of the 38 seasons between 1929 and 1966, the Yankees catching was, for the most part, handled by just three men: Dickey, Berra, and Howard. And in the 51-year period from 1929 through 1979, Dickey, Berra, Howard, and Munson did the bulk of the catching for the Yankees in 43 seasons. That's a pretty good run—just four men at the most demanding position on the field in 43 out of 51 years. I doubt if any other team has had that kind of continuity at the catching position.

In my own 16 years as a Yankee, with the exception of an occasional start by Charlie Silvera, Ralph Houk, Johnny Blanchard, or Jake Gibbs, I had only two catchers: Yogi Berra and Ellie Howard.

Some old-timers might question my choice of Berra over Dickey as the greatest of all Yankees catchers. Dickey had a lifetime batting average of .313, 28 points higher than Berra's, with a high of .362 in 1936. Berra's highest average was .307 in 1954. But that's the only category in which Dickey surpassed Berra.

Berra played more seasons (19 to Dickey's 17), hit more home runs (358 to Dickey's 202), and had more RBIs (1,430 to Dickey's 1,209). Berra had five 100 RBI seasons to Dickey's four, and Berra was the American League's Most Valuable Player three times.

It's possible that I lean toward Berra out of loyalty, because I saw him play so often. He was as good a clutch hitter and bad-ball hitter as I've ever seen. But I believe Berra's true value lay in how often he was a winner. In his 19 seasons, the Yankees won 14 pennants and 10 World Series. In Dickey's 17 seasons, the Yankees won 8 pennants and 7 World Series.

I'll never forget the first time I met Berra. It was late in the 1946 season, and I had just been signed by the Yankees. It turned out to be the first game Berra and Bobby Brown played for the team. They had just been called up from Newark to finish out the season with the big club.

Paul Krichell, the scout who signed me, introduced us. "Larry," he said, "I want you to meet Eddie Ford. He just signed with us. Eddie, this is Larry Berra." Yogi was still called "Larry" then, and I wouldn't be known as "Whitey" until I was in the minor leagues. Little did I know that Berra and I would share so many great times together in the future. Here it is more than 55 years later, and we're still the closest of friends.

Berra was my catcher in the first game I pitched for the Yankees in 1950, and he was my catcher for just about all my starts until 1958, when Ellie Howard came along and they began to ease him into Berra's job. Then Howard was my catcher for most of my starts until he was traded to the Red Sox in 1967, my final season.

When I was called up to the Yankees from Kansas City halfway into the 1950 season, the one guy I knew best on the team was Billy Martin. We had hung out during spring training and also in Kansas City, when Martin was sent down for a couple of weeks. But when I arrived to join the Yankees in

4

My No. 1 Yankees center fielder, Joe DiMaggio (left), and my No. 1 Yankees catcher, Yogi Berra, played together for five seasons, 1947 through 1951, and helped the Yankees win four World Series championships.

Boston, Martin already had a roommate, so they put me with Berra, who was rooming alone.

We were the original odd couple. Berra liked to go to bed early and wake up early. I liked to go to bed late and sleep late. As you can imagine, there were problems.

Berra was a creature of habit. He got up every morning at 6:00 and made sure he made enough noise to wake me up. He wanted to have a conversation while he got dressed, but I wanted to sleep. Then he'd finally leave the room and go downstairs to buy a newspaper and have breakfast. An hour or so later he'd come back to the room, making more noise and waking me up again, of course. Then he'd get back into bed and go to sleep, and I'd be wide-awake.

If I came back to the room late at night, the room would be dark. Berra would be in bed, and I figured he was asleep, so I wouldn't turn on the light. I would stumble around in the dark getting undressed, banging my toes. I'd get all ready for bed, go to the bathroom, then come back and quietly crawl into bed. As soon as I was in bed, Berra would turn on the light and want to start talking. He was awake the whole time.

Once, after I had been with the team for about a month, we were in Chicago and I was scheduled to pitch a day game. Berra went through his routine: getting up at 6:00, getting dressed, going down for the paper and breakfast. He wanted me to join him, but I told him no. "Let me sleep," I said. "I'm tired. But wake me up when you leave for the ballpark and I'll get up and take a cab out there."

He never called. All of a sudden, the phone rang. It was Red Patterson, our public relations director. "What the hell are you doing?" Patterson started shouting in my ear. "Don't you know you're pitching today? Casey's really mad."

I asked Patterson what time it was. "It's noon," he said. "The game is at 1:00."

I jumped out of bed and got dressed as quickly as I could. There wasn't even time for breakfast. Then I took a cab from the Del Prado Hotel to Comiskey Park. I arrived at the park at 12:30; I was supposed to start pitching at 1:00.

I ran into the clubhouse and started putting on my uniform. I finally got out on the field at 12:45 and began to warm up. My teeth were chattering, I was so scared.

To make me feel worse, a few old pros like Hank Bauer, Gene Woodling, and Allie Reynolds came over to me and said, "Hey, rookie, don't go fooling around with our money."

Fortunately, I won the game, 2–0, and everything turned out all right. When I asked Berra why he didn't wake me, he gave me one of his typical profound answers: "I forgot."

He might not have been the ideal roommate, but as a catcher Berra was the best. He was great at blocking balls in the dirt, which was a tremendous asset for a sinkerball pitcher like me. I knew I could throw the ball low and out of the strike zone trying to get the hitter to chase it, and not have to worry about it getting past Berra.

He was also brilliant at calling a game. His knowledge of the game and his ability to pick up hitters' strengths and weaknesses was uncanny. After a few weeks, we developed a pitcher-catcher rapport; we seemed to always be in sync with one another. I rarely had to shake him off, and usually when I did, it turned out Berra was right after all.

One time he wanted a fastball and I wanted a slow curve. I shook him off, threw the slow curve, and got beat on a home run. After the game, Berra came up to me and said, "Stick that slow curve up your ass." That's about the closest thing to a disagreement we have ever had in all the years we've known each other. I learned not to doubt him or his suggestions on pitch selection.

There was one time when I got beat on a pitch Berra called and Mickey Mantle got on Berra for his pitch selection. I didn't know it at the time, but after that game Mantle talked Berra into letting him call the pitches in my next start. So they worked out this system. If Mantle stood straight up, Berra would call for a fastball. If Mantle crouched with his hands on his knees, Berra would signal for a curve. If Mantle wanted me to throw a change-up, he'd waggle his glove.

This went on for seven innings. The score was 0–0 and Mantle was getting a little nervous, so he went to Berra and said, "I got you this far, you can take it the rest of the way."

I was too young when I saw **Bill Dickey** play to remember anything about him, but his record speaks for itself. And I've heard from many of his contemporaries about what a great catcher he was, in addition to being a dangerous left-handed hitter, especially in Yankee Stadium.

In 1937, Johnny Murphy (left), the first great relief pitcher for the Yankees, won 12 games in relief and saved 10. Bill Dickey (center) batted .332 and hit 29 home runs. Vernon "Lefty" Gomez led the American League with 21 wins, a 2.33 earned run average, 194 strikeouts, and six shutouts. I was eight years old at the time.

I got to know Dickey after he retired. When I joined the Yankees in 1950, he was the first-base coach and also what passed for a hitting instructor at that time. Things were different then. Stengel had only three coaches: Jim Turner, the pitching coach; Frank Crosetti, the third-base coach, who also worked with the infielders; and Dickey, who coached first base and worked with the hitters.

Back then we didn't have batting cages under the stands where players could get extra hitting practice, as they do now. We didn't have computer printouts or advance scouts or videotapes like the ones hitters now use when they're in a slump in order to see what they might be doing wrong. In fact, in my day, there wasn't a lot of batting practice like there is now. The players would take maybe 20 or 30 swings before a game, and that was it.

Dickey was a quiet man who didn't have a lot to say; he was a typical Southern gentleman from Bastrop, Louisiana. The thing that surprised

*"Bill Dickey is teaching me all his experiences."*
—Yogi Berra

me about him was his size, about 6′2″, which was big for a catcher, especially in his day. Probably his most important assignment as a coach for the Yankees was to help Berra improve as a catcher, which brought about one of Yogi's famous lines: "Bill Dickey is teaching me all his experiences."

To some degree, Berra taught Ellie Howard his "experiences" when Howard came along and was being groomed to replace Berra in 1955. Howard was traded in the middle of the 1967 season, and for a few years, Jake Gibbs did most of the catching. Then, in 1969, **Thurman Munson** came along. I had

Thurman Munson (shown here with Steve Garvey during the 1978 World Series) was one of the greatest competitors I've ever seen. He would have fit in perfectly with the teams I played for, but because Yogi Berra was our catcher, Munson would have had to move to another position.

retired by then, but I was a coach in 1974 and 1975 and got to see Munson up close on a daily basis.

Munson didn't look very smooth, and he didn't have a great arm, but he got rid of the ball very quickly. I never saw a catcher pick runners off first and third base the way he did. And he was one of the greatest competitors I've ever seen, a guy who hated to lose and would do whatever it took to win.

The one thing Munson didn't do was hit home runs, mainly because he played in Yankee Stadium, with its deep left-center field, known as Death Valley. Only once in his career did he hit 20 homers, but in three consecutive seasons, 1975 through 1977, he drove in at least 100 runs. I believe that if he and Carlton Fisk changed places so that Fisk had to hit in Yankee Stadium and Munson played in Fenway Park, Munson would be in the Hall of Fame today instead of Fisk.

*A* highlight of the 1976 World Series between the New York Yankees and the Cincinnati Reds was the confrontation between baseball's two premier catchers, Thurman Munson of the Yankees and Johnny Bench of the Reds.

The Yankees had returned to the World Series for the first time in 12 years with a renovated ballpark, a feisty and fiery manager, and a new cast of heroes.

In the 1974 and 1975 seasons, the Yankees played their home games at Shea Stadium, sharing the facility with the New York Mets while venerable and stately Yankee Stadium underwent a $100 million face-lift. The Yankees moved back into their renovated home in 1976, their first full year under new manager Billy Martin. He had been hired to replace Bill Virdon as manager the previous season—the prodigal son returning to the scene of his own World Series triumphs 20 years after he had been unceremoniously dumped in a trade.

With Martin came new Yankees heroes: Chris Chambliss, Willie Randolph, Graig Nettles, Catfish Hunter, Mickey Rivers, and Munson. They won the American League East by 10½ games over the Baltimore Orioles, then captured the American League pennant in a heart-stopping, five-game American League Championship Series with the Kansas City Royals.

In his seventh season, Munson attained stardom by batting .302, driving in 105 runs, and winning the American League's Most Valuable Player award. He hoped the World Series would provide him with a national forum to validate his star status.

The Cincinnati Reds were baseball's most powerful team, the "Big Red Machine." They had won the World Series in 1975, finished 10 games ahead of the Los Angeles Dodgers in the National League West in 1976, then swept the Philadelphia Phillies in the National League Championship Series. The Reds possessed a potent offense led by MVP Joe Morgan, Tony Perez, Pete Rose, George Foster, and Bench.

Although a series of minor injuries had curtailed his offense (he batted only .234, hit 16 home runs, and drove in 74 runs), Bench led the National League in home runs twice and in RBIs three times during the previous six seasons; he was regarded by many as the greatest catcher the game had ever known. And he was motivated in the World Series to "carry the team the way they carried me all season."

Munson achieved his personal objective by leading the Yankees with a .529 batting average, including hits in each of his last six at-bats in the Series. But he was no match for Bench, who batted .533, hit two home runs (Munson didn't hit any), and drove in six runs (Munson drove in two) in the Reds' four-game sweep of the Yankees.

In the press interview room following the final game, Reds' manager Sparky Anderson, intending to pay homage to his own man without disparaging Munson, made this comment: "Don't embarrass no catcher by comparing him to Johnny Bench." Sitting in the back of the room, Munson, a relentless competitor and a prideful man, was stung and visibly hurt by Anderson's remarks.

Said Sparky Anderson:

*I never said Munson couldn't catch or anything like that. My God, this guy could flat-out play, but I don't believe to this day you could compare anybody to Johnny Bench.*

*I was wired for the World Series film and there's one time I'm going to the mound to talk to my pitcher after Munson just got a hit and you hear me say, "That guy can flat-out hit."*

*The thing about him on our scouting report from Ray Shore was, "This guy can hit, let's don't worry about his hitting, let's keep him from going deep. Let's keep him in right and center field." And that's what we did. We pitched him so he could get all the hits he wanted to right field and right-center, but we weren't going to let him beat us by going deep to left. And he didn't. He hit over .500, but he never hurt us because we kept him there.*

*After the Series, I wrote him a letter, personally handwritten, explaining what I meant, and sent it to Yankee Stadium. He said he never got it, and that's fine. I'm not going to get into a media thing with him. I feel bad that he said he never got my letter because I had a lot of respect for Munson as a ballplayer, but I can understand a letter going to Yankee Stadium, some mail, let's face it, in the winter, you might not ever see your mail. And then it's all just put away and trashed.*

*He probably never did receive my letter. But I wrote it.*

But I always thought home runs were overrated, anyway. Mark McGwire and Sammy Sosa hit all those home runs, but I'd just as soon have a couple of Paul O'Neills, Bernie Williamses, and Thurman Munsons on my team.

**Ellie Howard**, No. 4 on my list of all-time Yankees catchers, joined us in 1955 after a terrific season with Toronto in the International League, where he batted .330 with 22 home runs and 109 RBIs. He was the first African American ever to play for the Yankees, and he was immediately accepted by everybody because he was such a good ballplayer and an equally good fellow. He and Berra became especially close because they both came from St. Louis.

Berra was still catching 140 games a year when Howard arrived, so Howard broke in playing a little outfield, a little first base, and occasionally catching. It wasn't until 1960 that he began catching more games than Berra. He was my primary catcher when I won 25 games in 1961 and again when I won 24 games in 1963.

I liked pitching to Howard. At 6′2″, he was six inches taller than Berra and made a better target. He also set up a foot or more closer to the batter than

Berra did; it made me feel like I was right on top of the batter. I threw a curveball that broke down sharply, and Howard would catch it a few inches off the ground; with Berra, it might hit the ground and I wouldn't get the strike call. I used to tell Berra to move up closer to the batter, but he said he was afraid of getting hit with a backswing.

And another thing: Berra used this big, old catcher's mitt that was so soft it was like throwing into cotton. I'd warm up in the bullpen and throw to our bullpen coach, Jim Hegan, a great catcher with the Cleveland Indians in his day. The ball would slam into his glove—bang, bang. Then I'd get in the game and it would go "poof" when it hit Berra's soft pillow. It didn't help my confidence or my ego.

Ellie Howard's mitt was like Hegan's. It was harder than Berra's, and the ball would bang into that glove with a crack that made me feel as if I was throwing the ball 95 miles an hour instead of my usual 85- or 87-mile-per-hour fastball.

Let me clarify one thing about Howard. He was often accused of cheating to help me win. There was a story going around the American League that he had filed down one of the clasps on his shin guard and that he rubbed the baseball against the filed-down clasp to cut the ball so that it would move a lot when I threw it. Everybody thought he was nicking the ball, but he wasn't; still, we kept the story alive by never denying it. I figured if the other teams thought he was cutting the baseball, that was one more thing the hitter had to worry about.

Howard was also the guy who gave me the nickname "Chairman of the Board." There was a disc jockey in New York at the time who pinned that name on Frank Sinatra. So Howard just adopted it and began calling me the "Chairman of the Board." I was flattered and honored to have the nickname.

As has been mentioned previously, in the almost 100-year history of the Yankees, four men did the bulk of their catching. A handful of other catchers held the job for at least three years, but none more than five seasons. Red Kleinow, Jeff Sweeney, Les Nunamaker, and Wally Schang all caught for the Yankees before I was born. In recent years, Jake Gibbs, Rick Cerone, Butch Wynegar, and Mike Stanley have each served as the Yankees regular catcher for at least three seasons. But, based on their records, it would be difficult to justify placing any of them in the No. 5 position.

Going into the 2001 season, the current Yankees catcher, **Jorge Posada**, had been with the team just four seasons, only three as the first stringer. But he had already done enough to make my all-time team at No. 5.

The 2000 season was a breakout one for Posada. He batted .287, drove in 86 runs, and belted 28 homers, more than any other Yankee catcher except Berra, who hit 30 home runs in 1952 and again in 1956. Posada also threw out 34 of 104 runners attempting to steal, an excellent 33 percent.

It may seem premature to rate Posada among the top five Yankees catchers in so short a time until you realize that in one season he hit more home runs than Kleinow, Sweeney, Schang, Nunamaker, Gibbs, and Wynegar did in their entire Yankees careers, and just three fewer than Cerone. And he figures to keep getting better.

When the 2001 season began, Posada was 29, just entering the prime years of his career. So there is good reason to believe that over the next few years, Posada will move up on the all-time list of Yankees catchers.

# Statistical Summaries

## HITTING

All statistics are for player's Yankees career only.

**G** = Games

**H** = Hits

**HR** = Home runs

**RBI** = Runs batted in

**SB** = Stolen bases

**BA** = Batting average

| Catcher | Years | G | H | HR | RBI | SB | BA |
|---|---|---|---|---|---|---|---|
| Yogi Berra<br><br>*Played in the most World Series games (75) and had most hits (71)* | 1946–63 | 2,116 | 2,148 | 358 | 1,430 | 30 | .285 |
| Bill Dickey<br><br>*Caught 100 or more games a record 13 consecutive seasons (1928–41)* | 1928–43<br>1946 | 1,789 | 1,969 | 202 | 1,209 | 36 | .313 |
| Thurman Munson<br><br>*Career batting average of .357 in 30 postseason games* | 1969–79 | 1,423 | 1,558 | 113 | 701 | 48 | .292 |

| (continued) | Years | G | H | HR | RBI | SB | BA |
|---|---|---|---|---|---|---|---|
| Elston Howard<br><br>*Tied with Bill Freehan for highest career fielding average (.993)* | 1955–67 | 1,492 | 1,405 | 161 | 733 | 8 | .279 |
| Jorge Posada<br><br>*Posada and Bernie Williams first team-mates to switch-hit homers in one game (April 4, 2000).* | 1995–2000 | 443 | 382 | 63 | 231 | 4 | .265 |

## FIELDING

Statistics are for player's entire career.

**PO** = Put-outs

**A** = Assists

**E** = Errors

**DP** = Double plays

**TC/G** = Total chances divided by games played

**FA** = Fielding average

| Catcher | PO | A | E | DP | TC/G | FA |
|---|---|---|---|---|---|---|
| Yogi Berra | 9,194 | 819 | 125 | 183 | 5.2 | .988 |
| Bill Dickey | 7,965 | 974 | 108 | 137 | 5.3 | .988 |
| Thurman Munson | 6,342 | 742 | 130 | 85 | 5.2 | .982 |
| Elston Howard | 7,572 | 541 | 68 | 160 | 5.5 | .992 |
| Jorge Posada | 2,642 | 173 | 20 | 29 | 6.6 | .993 |

# TWO

# First Baseman

I saw LOU GEHRIG PLAY, BUT I CAN'T tell you anything about it because I can't remember anything about it. I don't remember if I saw him hit a home run or drive in any runs. It's all a blank in my mind.

I just know I saw him play because I saw my first Yankees game in 1938 when I was nine, and that was Gehrig's final full season. Because he was in the last days of his streak of playing in 2,130 consecutive games, I know I had to have seen him play; he didn't miss any games in 1938.

In fact, Gehrig passed the 2,000 consecutive games mark that season, so for all I know I might have been there the day he played in his 2,000th consecutive game. But I don't know if that's the case. I just don't remember.

What I do know is that you didn't have to see Gehrig play to know that

1. LOU GEHRIG

2. DON MATTINGLY

3. MOOSE SKOWRON

4. CHRIS CHAMBLISS

5. TINO MARTINEZ

he belongs not only on any all-time Yankees team, he's at the top of the list of all-time Yankees first basemen. When you see any all-time baseball team, invariably Gehrig is the first baseman. And he will continue to be until Mark McGwire hits 800 career home runs.

I don't remember it, but I must have seen Lou Gehrig play when I saw my first Yankees game in 1938 because he was in the midst of his consecutive-game streak and he didn't miss any games that season. *Photo courtesy of the Baseball Hall of Fame.*

18

All you have to do is look at Gehrig's record—the 2,130 consecutive games, a lifetime batting average of .340, 493 career home runs, 1,990 career RBIs. Seven times he drove in more than 150 runs in a season, including an American League record of 184 in 1931. He drove in more than 100 runs in 13 consecutive seasons.

Five times he hit more than 40 home runs in a season, and I feel safe in saying that if it weren't for Babe Ruth, Gehrig would have been the great home-run hitter of his time. Take 1927, when Ruth hit his 60 homers. Gehrig hit 47 that year, and no other American League player hit more than 18. The following year, Ruth hit 54 homers, Gehrig 27, and no other American League player hit more than 17.

The other thing I know about Lou Gehrig is that, for a big guy, he could really run. He had 162 career triples including a league-leading 20 in 1926. He stole 102 bases in his career and holds the Yankees record for stealing home.

On a personal note, after my senior year in high school I played in a sand-lot league in New York. My team, the 34th Avenue Boys, was 36–0, and we won the Queens-Nassau championship. We were matched against a team from the Bronx for the New York sandlot championship, sponsored by a

If there had never been a Babe Ruth, Lou Gehrig—"The Iron Horse"—would have been regarded as the greatest home-run hitter of his generation. *Photo courtesy of the Baseball Hall of Fame.*

newspaper, the New York *Journal-American*. I pitched the game, and we went to the tenth inning tied 0–0. In the top of the tenth I led off with a double and scored the only run. I was named the game's Most Valuable Player and was presented with the Lou Gehrig Trophy. And how's this for a coincidence? Twenty-four years later, my son Eddie won the same trophy.

*"Don Mattingly was the best-fielding first baseman I ever saw in a Yankees uniform."*
—WHITEY FORD

The one thing statistics don't tell us is how good a defensive first baseman Gehrig was. I have heard from those who saw him that he was very good, but I can't imagine him being better than **Don Mattingly**, the best-fielding first baseman I ever saw in a Yankees uniform. He made the first-short-first double play better than anybody I've ever seen.

Being a left-handed thrower gave Mattingly an edge over the great first basemen of my day, like Gil Hodges and Vic Power, the fanciest first baseman I've ever seen.

I never saw a better defensive first baseman in a Yankees uniform than Don Mattingly.

In 1987, Don Mattingly belted six grand slams and set major league records with nine home runs in seven consecutive games and ten home runs in eight consecutive games. Here he's greeted after a home run by Willie Randolph (right), who makes my list of all-time Yankees second basemen. That's a former Yankee, Orioles catcher Rick Dempsey, on the left.

Mattingly had the misfortune of playing on teams that made it to the post-season just once in his 14 years as a Yankee. That was in his last year, 1995, when the Yankees were eliminated by the Seattle Mariners in the division playoff series. So, Mattingly is one of the few truly great players in baseball history who never played in a World Series.

But he finished his career among the top 10 Yankees in games played, at-bats, runs, hits (fifth behind Gehrig, Ruth, Mantle, and DiMaggio with 2,153), doubles (second to Gehrig), home runs (222), RBIs (1,099), and batting average (.307).

In a four-year period, from 1984 through 1987, he was regarded as the best player in the game. During that period, Mattingly won a batting title, led the American League in hits and doubles in 1984, led the league in RBIs with 145, hit 35 home runs, and was named Most Valuable Player in 1985. He batted .352 and led the league in hits (238) and doubles (53) in 1986. He set major league records with 9 home runs in seven consecutive games, 10 home runs in eight consecutive games, and 6 grand slams for the season in 1987.

But it was on defense that Mattingly really made his mark. When he retired, he had received nine Gold Gloves, led American League first basemen in fielding percentage seven times (a record), and held the major league record for fielding percentage at any position with .996.

The only Yankees first baseman I've ever seen who even came close to Mattingly defensively was Joe Pepitone, who could have been one of the greatest Yankees ever if he paid a little more attention to playing. I'm not telling tales out of school; in his own book, Pepi admitted that he wasted his talent with his loose lifestyle.

Pepitone had so much ability, but he let his off-field behavior get in his way. In 1964, his second season with us, he knocked in 100 runs and hit 28 home runs. Two years later, he hit 31 home runs. In 1967, when Mickey Mantle was injured, Pepi played the best center field I saw from a Yankee since Joe DiMaggio or Mantle.

Pepitone was a fun guy and a great teammate, and he provided some of the fondest memories I have in my career. He was the first guy I ever saw using a hair dryer in the clubhouse. Pepi was a streetwise kid from Brooklyn, which is probably why I took to him so easily. We had similar upbringings. He was brash and bold and very cocky.

During Mantle's last season, 1968, we went to Detroit, and Mickey was tied with Jimmie Foxx at 534 for third on the all-time home-run list. Denny McLain started for the Tigers, and he was having a tremendous year. He would win 31 games that season. Late in the game, we were losing by about six runs when Mantle came to bat for the last time. As he stepped into the batter's box, McLain called his catcher, Jim Price, to the mound and said, loud enough for Mickey to hear, "This is probably his last time at bat in Detroit. Let's let him hit one."

Mantle couldn't believe what he was hearing. "Hey, Jim," he said to Price, "did I hear what I think I heard? He wants me to hit one."

Defensively, the Yankees' infield of (from left) third baseman Clete Boyer, shortstop Tony Kubek, second baseman Bobby Richardson, and first baseman Joe Pepitone, who played together from 1963 through 1965, was as good as they come.

"Yeah," Price said. "He's not going to work on you. He's just going to throw you fastballs."

Mantle must have been skeptical because he let the first fastball go by. And McLain just looked at him as if to say, "Hey, what are you looking at?"

Now Mantle knew McLain wasn't trying to set him up. He was serious. He was going to lay it right in for Mick. And that's what he did on the next pitch, and Mantle hit it into the upper deck to pass Foxx with the 535th home run of his career.

Let me say that even when he knows what's coming, there's no guarantee a batter is going to hit it out. How many times have you seen guys try to hit home runs in batting practice, or in home run–hitting contests, and not be able to do it? So don't take anything away from Mantle just because McLain laid one in for him.

Pepitone was the batter after Mantle. He had been watching all this and figured McLain was in a generous mood. Being the free spirit he is, Pepitone motioned to McLain with his right hand over the middle of the plate, as if to say, "I'll take one right here." Instead, McLain threw a fastball up and in and knocked Pepi on his ass.

Then there was the famous "Harmonica Incident" in Chicago in 1964. Berra was the manager, and we had just lost a doubleheader to the White Sox in late August that dropped us six and a half games out of first place. It looked like we were dead.

Phil Linz, a utility infielder, had bought a harmonica in Chicago and was teaching himself how to play. So Linz is sitting in the back of the bus trying to play "Mary Had a Little Lamb" when Berra, still burning over losing the doubleheader, comes onto the bus. He hears Linz and shouts at him, "Hey, Linz, stuff that harmonica."

Linz turns to Mantle and says, "What did he say?"

Mantle tells him, "He said play louder."

So Linz plays it again.

Now Berra comes charging to the back of the bus, and he's really pissed. "I told you to stick that harmonica up your ass."

With that, Linz flips the harmonica at Berra, Mantle swats it with his hand, and it hits Pepitone on the knee. Now, Pepi jumps up screaming, "Oh, my knee. I'm injured."

All the papers made a big thing out of the incident. Berra fined Linz, then later the fine was rescinded. Linz even got an endorsement from the harmonica company. And we wound up winning the pennant, and a lot of people pointed to the harmonica incident as the turning point, kind of a rallying point.

I was sitting in the back of the bus near Mantle when the whole thing broke out. When Mantle slapped the harmonica and it hit Pepitone's knee and fell to the floor, I picked it up and stuck it in my pocket. I still have that harmonica at home in my den.

24

Another time, Pepitone was playing first base in the 1963 World Series against the Dodgers. I lost the first game in Yankee Stadium, 5–2, when Sandy Koufax struck out 15 of our hitters. We lost the second game at home, then we lost the third game in Los Angeles.

Now it was my turn again in Game 4 in Los Angeles, an afternoon game, and it was up to me to keep us alive in the Series. Again, I was matched with Koufax.

After four innings, the game was scoreless. We had one hit off Koufax, who struck out four. They had one hit off me. In the bottom of the fifth, Frank Howard hit a tremendous home run off me to give the Dodgers a 1–0 lead. Mantle homered in the top of the seventh to tie the score, 1–1.

Then in the bottom of the seventh, Junior Gilliam hit a ground ball to Clete Boyer at third. He fielded it cleanly and threw across to Pepitone, and the ball hit Pepi in the wrist and ricocheted down into the right-field corner. Gilliam reached third and scored on Willie Davis' sacrifice fly. Later, Pepi said he lost the ball in the white shirts of the fans sitting behind third base. We ended up losing the game 2–1, although I gave up only two hits.

After the game I went up to Pepitone at his locker, where he was sitting with his chin on his chest, all upset because he cost us the game. I think he expected me to pat him on the back and say, "That's OK, kid, those things happen," or something comforting like that. I wouldn't give him the satisfaction. Instead, I figured I'd have a little fun with him. "Well, you sure blew that one," I said with a straight face, pretending to be serious.

During the World Series, the *New York Daily News* picks a hero and a goat for each game. There would be two cartoons in the paper the next day, one of the hero of the game with a halo around his head, the other of the goat with a pair of goat horns. So I really laid it on. I told Pepitone, "You're going to be the goat tomorrow in the *Daily News*."

Here it is almost 30 years later, and I still bring it up to Pepitone occasionally. I think he finally realizes I was just needling him.

Pepitone joined us in 1962 and showed such promise that after the season we traded **Moose Skowron** to the Dodgers. Skowron makes my list of all-time Yankees first basemen at No. 3.

The first time I ever saw Skowron was 1950, my rookie season. That same year I saw Mickey Mantle for the first time. Skowron was 19, a kid out of

Chicago, and he had signed a contract with the Yankees after his freshman year at Purdue, where he was a punter on the football team. Mantle was 18 and had just finished his second year of pro ball with class A Joplin, where he batted .383 with 26 homers and 136 RBIs. The Yankees wanted to take a close look at Mantle and Skowron and another kid, Kal Segrist, one of the first of baseball's bonus babies.

The Yankees gave Segrist a signing bonus of $50,000, which was a fortune in those days. But he played only two seasons in the major leagues. Mantle signed for $500 and played eighteen seasons.

The first time I saw Bill "Moose" Skowron was in 1950. He was 19 years old and had just signed with the Yankees out of Purdue University, where he was a punter on the football team. Skowron was my teammate for nine of my sixteen seasons with the Yankees.

The three of them were invited to join us on a road trip to St. Louis and Chicago. They would stay a few weeks, taking batting practice and getting to experience life in the big leagues.

Skowron came to the Yankees in 1954 and slowly moved in to replace Joe Collins as our first baseman. He took over the job full time in 1956, and for the next seven years, he was one of our steadiest players. He was a strong, right-handed hitter who learned how to drive the ball to right field in Yankee Stadium, where the fences were more reachable than they were in left.

Skowron hit for a good average, .282 lifetime, and knocked in a lot of runs. He was consistently in the 23- to 28-home-run range with 80 to 90 RBIs and a batting average around .300. And he worked hard to be the best defensive first baseman he could be.

Skowron was one of the meanest looking guys you'd ever want to see, but he was also one of the sweetest, gentlest people you'd ever meet. He could be tough if you crossed him, but he was usually easygoing.

Mantle used to try to get him to come out with us, but he always refused. He kept insisting it was nothing personal, he just had a different, more quiet lifestyle.

We finally talked him into going out with us during spring training in 1961. First, we set it up with our manager, Ralph Houk. Mantle and I told Houk we wanted to take Skowron out, and Houk gave us the OK.

We rented a limousine and picked him up and handed him a chauffeur's cap and told him he was to be our chauffeur for the night. He played along with us. He'd open the back door for us, then run around to the driver's seat and drive us around wearing his little cap. We hit all the hot spots and wound up bowling, and we didn't get home until 2:00 A.M. And we had a day game that day in Clearwater.

Houk wrote Skowron's name into the starting lineup. I thought he was going to get sick on the field during infield practice, he was so hungover.

He told Mantle, "Mick, I can't play today."

"You have to, Moose," Mantle said. "You can't tell Houk you were out all night. He'll go crazy and fine you."

Of course, we had it all set up with Houk, and when the game started, Houk took Skowron out of the lineup. The three of us spent the game sitting along the fence and dozing off. That was the last time he ever went out with us, but he and I stayed close, and we remain friends to this day.

*I*n 1951 the Yankees signed 19-year-old Bill "Moose" Skowron from Purdue University for the then-substantial bonus of $5,000 and sent him to their Binghamton farm team, where he played only 21 games before being shipped to Norfolk.

In 95 games with Norfolk, Skowron batted .334 with 18 home runs and 78 RBIs, which earned him a promotion to the Yankees' top farm team, in Kansas City. It was in Kansas City during 1952 that the Yankees realized they had something special in the powerfully built first baseman, who batted .341 with a league-leading 31 homers and 134 runs batted in.

Unfortunately for Skowron, veteran Joe Collins was solidly entrenched as the Yankees first baseman. So rather than have the youngster come to New York and sit on the bench, the Yankees let him spend a second consecutive season in Kansas City, where he again batted over .300. Although his power numbers and run production dropped off from the previous season, Skowron was still a highly regarded prospect by the Yankees, who brought him up to the big club in 1954. It wasn't until two seasons later, however, that Skowron took over as the Yankees' regular first baseman, a position he held for seven productive seasons.

By his own account, Skowron was "no gazelle" at first base, but he worked hard and became more than adequate at the position. It was his bat that made him a valuable member of a team that won seven American League pennants and four World Series in his nine seasons in New York. He batted over .300 five times, hit more than 20 home runs four times, and twice drove in 90 runs or more.

After the 1962 season, with the Yankees in need of pitching help and eager to make room for left-handed hitter Joe Pepitone, a highly regarded power prospect, Skowron was traded to the Los Angeles Dodgers for Stan Williams.

Said Skowron, "The trade broke my heart. I was no Dodger. I was a Yankee. I'm still a Yankee. I'll always be a Yankee. I was a Yankee for twelve years. I was a Dodger for one."

Skowron's year as a Dodger wasn't a very good one. Platooning with Ron Fairly at first base, he played in only 89 games, batted .203, hit four home runs, and drove in only 19 runs. They were hardly the numbers people had come to expect from the man called "Moose."

It was with mixed emotions that Skowron played against his old friends and teammates:

> *We won the National League pennant and now we had to play the Yankees in the World Series, and that was a weird feeling, playing against my old team. All the guys I knew so well. I got hot in the World Series. In the first game, I got a couple of hits off Whitey [Ford] and drove in two runs. The next day, I hit a home run off Al Downing. I wound up hitting .385 in the Series, and we swept the Yankees in four games.*
>
> *That was the Series when Clete Boyer threw a ball from third base and Pepitone lost it in the shirts and it hit him in the wrist and cost them a game. I didn't get any satisfaction out of that. I felt bad for Pepi. I knew what it was like to try to pick the ball out of the white shirts in a day game.*
>
> *I never held it against Pepi that I was traded and he took my place. I understood the trade. Pepitone had all the God-given ability in the world. The one thing that bothered me is that I never heard from Ralph Houk that I was traded. When I saw him I said, "Why didn't you tell me I was traded?" He said, "Moose, it's a cold business. We just felt we had to make room for the young guy."*
>
> *After the 1963 World Series, I told Mickey [Mantle], "I wish I had been on the losing team." Mickey never forgot that. He mentioned it to me a few times. I meant it. I grew up with those guys. We had a family over there. Mickey, Whitey, Ellie, Yogi, Roger. We were like family and that's probably why we won so often.*

I was a coach for the Yankees in 1974 when they made the trade with Cleveland to get **Chris Chambliss**. I didn't like the trade at the time for selfish reasons. I was the pitching coach and we traded away half of our pitching staff—Fritz Peterson, Steve Kline, Fred Beene, and Tom Buskey—to get Chambliss.

The home run Chris Chambliss hit against the Kansas City Royals in the fifth game of the American League Championship Series to win the 1976 pennant was one of the biggest in Yankees history.

After a while, Chambliss began to grow on me, and it turned out to be one of the best trades the Yankees ever made. Chambliss was a steady, sure-handed first baseman and a productive and reliable hitter, especially in the clutch. He hit one of the biggest, most memorable and dramatic home runs in Yankees' history—the one that beat the Kansas City Royals in the bottom of the ninth inning of the final game of the 1976 American League Championship Series, which gave the Yankees their first pennant in 12 years. Chambliss is the original "Quiet Man," a guy who didn't say much, never complained, and just went out and did his job efficiently and without fanfare.

**Tino Martinez** is another player in that same mold. You had to feel for Martinez, replacing a great Yankees hero and fan favorite like Don Mattingly. At first, Martinez went through some tough times, being compared to Mattingly, unable to win the fans' approval. He eventually won them over in his second season with the Yankees when he belted 44 home runs, drove in 141 runs, and helped the Yankees win three world championships in four years.

Tino Martinez had some big shoes to fill when he replaced fan favorite Don Mattingly at first base in 1996. But he won over the fans by hitting 69 home runs and driving in 258 runs during his first two seasons as a Yankee.

# Statistical Summaries

## HITTING

All statistics are for player's Yankees career only.

**G** = Games

**H** = Hits

**HR** = Home runs

**RBI** = Runs batted in

**SB** = Stolen bases

**BA** = Batting average

| First Baseman | Years | G | H | HR | RBI | SB | BA |
|---|---|---|---|---|---|---|---|
| Lou Gehrig<br>*First of only three A.L. players to hit four homers in a game (June 3, 1932)* | 1923–39 | 2,164 | 2,721 | 493 | 1,990 | 102 | .340 |
| Don Mattingly<br>*Hit record six grand slams in 1987—the only six of his career* | 1982–95 | 1,785 | 2,153 | 222 | 1,099 | 14 | .307 |
| Moose Skowron<br>*All-Star selection five consecutive seasons (1957–61)* | 1954–62 | 1,087 | 1,103 | 165 | 672 | 14 | .294 |

| (continued) | Years | G | H | HR | RBI | SB | BA |
|---|---|---|---|---|---|---|---|
| Chris Chambliss<br><br>*Played 150 or more games in seven seasons, four while with Yanks* | 1974–79<br>1988 | 885 | 954 | 79 | 454 | 10 | .282 |
| Tino Martinez<br><br>*Has averaged 115 RBIs per season as a Yankee* | 1996–2000 | 769 | 801 | 141 | 577 | 14 | .278 |

## FIELDING

Statistics are for player's entire career.

**PO** = Put-outs

**A** = Assists

**E** = Errors

**DP** = Double plays

**TC/G** = Total chances divided by games played

**FA** = Fielding average

| First Baseman | PO | A | E | DP | TC/G | FA |
|---|---|---|---|---|---|---|
| Lou Gehrig | 19,525 | 1,087 | 196 | 1,574 | 9.7 | .991 |
| Don Mattingly | 14,625 | 1,120 | 68 | 1504 | 8.6 | .996 |
| Moose Skowron | 12,152 | 930 | 110 | 1,266 | 8.9 | .992 |
| Chris Chambliss | 17,771 | 1,351 | 130 | 1,687 | 9.7 | .993 |
| Tino Martinez | 9,936 | 773 | 56 | 924 | 8.9 | .995 |

## THREE

# Second Baseman

As with Lou Gehrig and Bill Dickey, I didn't have to see **Tony Lazzeri** play to know that he belongs on any all-time Yankees team. Lazzeri was the second baseman for the great Yankees' "Murderers Row" of the late twenties. He came to the Yankees in 1926, two years before I was born, but I heard a lot about Lazzeri from Frank Crosetti, who was the third-base coach for most of my years with the Yankees, and who, like Lazzeri, came from San Francisco. He played shortstop alongside Lazzeri in the thirties.

All you really have to do to appreciate Lazzeri is look at his record. He's the only Yankees second baseman in the Hall of Fame, and no wonder. In 14 seasons in the major leagues (12 with the Yankees), Lazzeri had a lifetime batting average of .292, 178 home runs, and 1,191 RBIs.

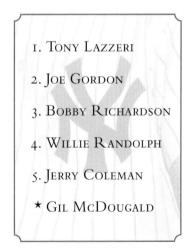

1. Tony Lazzeri

2. Joe Gordon

3. Bobby Richardson

4. Willie Randolph

5. Jerry Coleman

★ Gil McDougald

He had his best year in 1929, with a .354 batting average, 18 home runs, and 101 RBIs. The following year he batted .303 and hit 9 homers but raised his RBI total to 121. He would drive in 100 or more runs seven times in his career, bat over .300 five times, and hit 13 or more home runs nine times.

36

I never saw "Poosh 'em up" Tony Lazzeri play, but people who did tell me he was as good a second baseman as Rogers Hornsby, Frankie Frisch, or Charlie Gehringer. Lazzeri once hit 60 home runs in the minor leagues and is the only Yankees second baseman in the Hall of Fame. *Photo courtesy of the Baseball Hall of Fame.*

You might not think 13 is a lot of home runs by today's standards, but back then it was, believe me. For example, in 1926, when Lazzeri hit 18 homers, only Babe Ruth and Al Simmons hit more in the American League. And in 1927, when Lazzeri again hit 18, only Ruth and Gehrig hit more. Lazzeri also once hit 60 home runs in the minor leagues.

Lazzeri was at the forefront of a long and glorious tradition of Italian Americans playing for the Yankees. Their presence was largely responsible for introducing America's game to millions of first- and second-generation Italian Americans.

For six seasons, from 1932 through 1937, Frank Crosetti played alongside Tony Lazzeri in the Yankees infield, Crosetti the shortstop, Lazzeri the second baseman. Lazzeri, seven years older, was Crosetti's teammate, double-play partner, friend, and mentor. They were both infielders, both from San Francisco, both of Italian heritage. And they were both Yankees.

"Lazzeri was a great ballplayer," said Crosetti, whose career with the Yankees as a player and coach spanned five decades. "A great hitter, a great fielder. And a great guy. Very humble. You'd never hear Tony pop off. He wouldn't talk much. You'd hardly know he was around. When I was called up by the Yankees, I looked up Tony at his home, and he took me under his wing. He told me what to expect when I joined the team. He was a big help to me."

As a player, Lazzeri was in the shadow of his better-known teammates, Babe Ruth and Lou Gehrig, and of the star second basemen of his day, Charlie Gehringer in Detroit, Rogers Hornsby in St. Louis, and Frank Frisch with the New York Giants.

Crosetti said:

*Tony never complained that these other guys got more attention. He was as good a second baseman as any of them. Gehringer, Hornsby, and Frisch hit for a higher average, but Tony was a great hitter with power, especially to right-center. He could hit the long ball. He hit 60 home runs in Salt Lake City and still holds the Pacific Coast League record. He wasn't much bigger than me [Lazzeri 5'11½", 175 pounds, Crosetti 5'11", 165 pounds], but he was strong and thick through the chest with big arms and shoulders from working in the iron works foundry.*

*The Italian American people in New York loved him. He introduced baseball to a lot of Italian Americans, and they used to shout "Poosh 'em up, Tony," which meant push another run across the plate.*

*As a fielder, he was smooth and tough. He wasn't afraid to get his uniform dirty. One time, he let a ball go through his legs, and he was so mad at himself, and so determined not to let another ball go through his legs, the next time a ball was hit to him, he fielded it and picked up everything on the ground—dirt, gravel, pebbles—and threw it all to first base with the ball.*

Despite his quiet demeanor, Lazzeri often showed his impish side, according to Crosetti. He did it once at the expense of the mighty Babe Ruth, with whom Lazzeri enjoyed a warm relationship.

*Babe used to use this eye fluid called "Eye Low." He'd keep a bottle of it in the dugout, and he'd put it in his eyes when he was due to bat. One day, Tony poured out all the "Eye Low" and filled the bottle with water and sat waiting for the right time to pull his trick. He mentioned to Babe that his eyes were bothering him and Babe picked up the bottle of "Eye Low" and told Tony, "Here, try some of this."*

*Tony takes the bottle, uncaps it, and drinks it down. Babe almost had a heart attack.*

*"No, no," he's shouting. "You don't drink it; that's poison."*

Four years after Crosetti became a Yankee, in 1936, he and Lazzeri were joined on the team by another Italian American from San Francisco, a 21-year-old outfield sensation named Joe DiMaggio.

"The reason the Yankees got so many players out of San Francisco," said Crosetti, "is that they had two great scouts in the area, Bill Essick and Joe Devine. They signed most of us."

In the spring of 1936, Lazzeri and Crosetti decided that instead of taking the train from California to Florida, they would drive in Lazzeri's new

Buick sedan. They invited young DiMaggio to go with them. Crosetti remembered:

> We would share the driving and the expenses. I was in charge of the money. We each put up so much money for meals and gas and headed to Florida for spring training. There were no superhighways in those days. We had to go up hills and on winding roads and through towns. The trip took us about a week, with me and Tony doing all of the driving. None of us talked a lot, so on the whole drive, we probably didn't say more than three words to each other in a week.
>
> Just as we were reaching Florida, Tony said to me, "Let's make the kid drive."
>
> And the kid, DiMag, said, "I don't know how to drive."

Tony Lazzeri was released by the Yankees and picked up by the Cubs in 1938. He finished his career in 1939 with the Dodgers and Giants. He managed briefly in the minor leagues, then left baseball. He was elected to the Hall of Fame in 1991, 52 years after he retired.

"I always wondered why it took so long for him to get elected," Crosetti said. "He deserved to get in long before that. I'm just sorry he wasn't around to enjoy it."

Lazzeri died in 1946 at the age of 42.

The first Italian American to play for the Yankees, in fact the first Italian American to play in the major leagues, was an outfielder named Ping Bodie, whose real name was Francesco Stephano Pezzolo. He came out of San Francisco and started his major league career in 1911 with the Chicago White Sox. He was traded to the Philadelphia Athletics in 1917, then to the Yankees in 1918, and was the first of a string of Italian Americans from the San Francisco area who played for the Yankees.

Lazzeri came to the Yankees in 1926, then Crosetti came in 1932, then Joe DiMaggio in 1936. In later years, Billy Martin and Dave Righetti, two more Italian Americans from the San Francisco area, also played for the Yankees. The tradition of Italian Americans playing for the Yankees continued with Marius Russo, Phil Rizzuto, Vic Raschi, Yogi Berra, Joe Pepitone, all the way to Joe Torre, their current manager.

The neighborhood where I grew up—Astoria, Queens—was a melting pot of Irish Americans, German Americans, Swedish Americans, and Italian Americans. A few prominent Italian Americans came from my neighborhood. One was Sam Mele, a star baseball and basketball player at New York University who was inducted into the New York University Hall of Fame and played 10 seasons in the major leagues. Later, he managed the Minnesota Twins all the way to the 1965 American League pennant. Another prominent Italian American from my neighborhood was Anthony Benedetto, better known as Tony Bennett, the singer. Then there were Tony and Al Cuccinello. Tony played 15 years in the major leagues as an infielder with the Reds, Dodgers, Braves, Giants, and White Sox, and for many years he was the third-base coach for the Indians and White Sox. His brother, Al, played only one season with the Giants but spent many years as a scout for the Yankees.

*"Gehringer . . . Hornsby . . . Frisch. . . . Tony Lazzeri was as good a second baseman as any of them."*
—FRANK CROSETTI

I can tell you from personal experience that many people in my neighborhood who had come from Italy, could hardly speak English, and knew nothing about baseball when they arrived in this country became Yankees fans because of players like Crosetti, DiMaggio, and Lazzeri.

**Joe Gordon** was gone by the time I came to the Yankees. He joined them in 1938 and was traded nine years later to the Cleveland Indians for Allie Reynolds, one of those rare trades that helped both teams. With Gordon, the Indians won the World Series in 1948. Reynolds, who I'll talk more about later, helped the Yankees win five consecutive world championships from 1949 through 1953.

Gordon's last year in the majors was my first, 1950. So I played against him and against the three teams he managed, the Cleveland Indians, the Detroit Tigers, and the Kansas City Athletics. He was also part of one of the most bizarre trades in baseball history. On August 10, 1960, the Indians and Tigers swapped managers. Gordon went from Cleveland to Detroit, and Jimmy Dykes from Detroit to Cleveland.

When Gordon joined the Yankees, the top second baseman in the American League was future Hall of Famer Charlie Gehringer of Detroit. Soon, as Gehringer's career was winding down, the top second basemen in the league were Gordon and Bobby Doerr of the Boston Red Sox.

By the time I reached the major leagues in 1950, Joe Gordon had been traded by the Yankees and was playing for the Cleveland Indians. In his seven seasons as a Yankee, he hit 153 home runs, more than any other Yankees second baseman except Hall of Famer Tony Lazzeri.

*Photo courtesy of the Baseball Hall of Fame.*

Gordon was one of the best slugging second basemen of all time. In his 11 seasons, he belted 253 homers, an average of 23 a year. Twice he hit 30 or more with a high of 32 in 1948. Four times he drove in more than 100 runs, with a high of 124 in 1948. In his 14 seasons, Doerr never hit 40 homers, even though he was a right-handed hitter playing half his games in Fenway Park. He did drive in 100 runs six times, but never as many as 124 in a season. But Bobby Doerr is in the Hall of Fame, and Joe Gordon is not.

**Bobby Richardson** and Willie Randolph were very similar players. Both were complete professionals and outstanding defensive second basemen who were especially good at turning the double play. Both were excellent at doing the little things that don't show up in the box score but help you win ball games—get on base, bunt, steal a base, hit behind the runner—team players all the way.

During the 1960 season, Bobby Richardson drove in only 26 runs in 150 games, but he knocked in a record 6 runs in the third game of the World Series against the Pirates. I pitched a four-hit shutout in that game. We outscored the Pirates, 55–27, in the Series, but lost in seven games. I always believed we should have won that Series.

Both played about the same number of years, 13 seasons as a Yankee for Randolph, 12 for Richardson, who never played for another team. Randolph was a little faster and had more pop in his bat. He hit for a higher average than Richardson, had a few more home runs, a few more RBIs, and more stolen bases.

But Richardson once had 209 hits in a season and was at his best in big games. As an example, in 36 World Series games, he batted .305, 39 points higher than his regular season average. He set a record for the most hits in a five-game World Series with 9 in 1961 and tied the record for most hits in a seven-game World Series with 13 in 1964.

Richardson's greatest attribute probably was his durability. In a six-year period, from 1961 through 1966, he came to bat more than 600 times in each season, and he missed only 31 of the team's 1,028 games.

Richardson retired after the 1966 season. He had had a decent season, a .251 average, 42 RBIs, 71 runs, and his usual outstanding play at second base, only 15 errors. He was only 31 years old at the time, and he easily could have played another three or four years, at least.

We weren't making the kind of money then that they make today, but Richardson was paid very well for the time, and a lot of players would have hung on just for the money. Not Richardson. Money was never very important to him. He was a man of principle, a good family man who was tired of the travel and of being away from his family. And he had more important things he wanted to do with his life. Eventually, he coached baseball at the University of South Carolina and went into the ministry. To give you an idea of how highly I thought of Richardson, I sent my son Eddie to play for him at South Carolina.

Because Richardson was a man of such high moral standards, an incident that happened in the 1958 season was as amusing as it was ridiculous.

We were going bad that season, and Casey Stengel thought there was too much nightlife among the players on the club. He was right, but I'm not going to name names of the main culprits. The club hired a private detective to follow us around and report back to Stengel which players were breaking curfew. The whole thing got ridiculous at times.

The detective was no Columbo. He wore white rabbit-skin shoes, and you could spot him a mile away. Some detective! We would do funny things to drive this guy crazy. We'd walk out one door of the Statler Hilton in Detroit, for instance, get in a cab, and have the driver go around the corner and park in front of another entrance to the hotel. Our detective would be looking all over town for us.

Once he followed Tony Kubek, Bobby Shantz, and Bobby Richardson, who were three of the cleanest-living players we had. Richardson, especially, was very religious, but he never wore his religion on his sleeve. We all respected him for that, and he was one of the most well liked players on the team.

Our detective didn't know that, and one night Kubek, Shantz, and Richardson left the hotel and the detective followed them. They walked several blocks through the streets of Detroit, the detective trailing them every step of the way. He followed them right to the local YMCA, where they had gone to play Ping-Pong. You can bet that was one report that wasn't submitted to Stengel.

Maybe it's just a coincidence that the Yankees won their first American League pennant in 12 years in 1976, the year **Willie Randolph** arrived, but I don't think so. Randolph came from Pittsburgh in one of the greatest trades the Yankees ever made. They sent George "Doc" Medich, who helped save my life, to the Pirates for Randolph and pitchers Ken Brett (George's older brother) and Dock Ellis.

At the time, Randolph was just 21. He had played in 30 games with the Pirates in 1975 and showed promise, but he was blocked at second base in Pittsburgh by Rennie Stennett. The Pirates desperately needed pitching, and Medich, only 27 at the time, had won 49 games for the Yankees in the three previous seasons. Besides, he was from Aliquippa, Pennsylvania, a suburb of Pittsburgh.

I mentioned that Medich helped save my life. That happened in 1975, while I was the Yankees' pitching coach. We were playing our home games in Shea Stadium while Yankee Stadium was being renovated.

It was early in the season, May, but it was a hot, humid, steamy day in New York. We had a night game scheduled, but we all came out early for extra hitting. I was pitching batting practice and was supposed to throw for 15 minutes and then Ellie Howard would take over. But Howard said he had an upset stomach, so I told him not to worry, that I'd take his 15 minutes, too.

I was pitching to Lou Piniella; my second 15 minutes was just about up, and I started getting dizzy on the mound. Piniella could see there was something wrong. He stepped out of the cage and asked me if I was all right.

Mrs. Rachel Robinson and Willie Randolph mark 40 years since Jackie Robinson broke the color barrier in the major leagues.

Willie Randolph was a magician at turning the double play. Here he is as the middleman of a twin killing against the Indians. That's former Indians manager and current Orioles manager Mike Hargrove trying unsuccessfully to break up the DP.

Another coach, Dick Howser, came out to the mound and told me to stop throwing and go into the clubhouse.

I left the mound and headed for the dressing room. There's a long runway at Shea that leads from the home team's dugout to the clubhouse. As soon as I got down the steps into the runway, I passed out. I don't know how long I lay there. A security guard found me and called Gene Monahan, the trainer. It was fortunate that Medich, who was attending medical school in the off-season, came over to assist Monahan. I had pains in my chest and my arm.

I was taken to Long Island Jewish Hospital, where they gave me a complete physical and kept me there for a few days.

After I got out of the hospital, I got a telephone call from my old teammate, Bobby Brown. Dr. Bobby Brown. He was a well-known cardiologist in Fort Worth, Texas, at the time, and he told me to come down and he would give me a thorough examination. Brown took a lot of tests and found that no operation was necessary. I haven't had any trouble since then.

While I was in the hospital in Fort Worth, I got a call from another old teammate, Eddie Lopat.

"Whatever you do," Eddie said, "don't let that guy operate on you. Not with his hands. Did you ever see him play third base?"

Anyway, Willie Randolph came from the Pirates and joined the Yankees in spring training in 1976. He moved right in and took over the second-base job and kept it for 13 years. He was a natural. He had grown up in Brooklyn and was another of those street-smart city kids. He also was a thorough professional.

In his 13 seasons, the Yankees won four pennants and two World Series. When he finished his career, Randolph had played more games, had more at-bats, and scored more runs than any other Yankees second baseman. And he was second on the Yankees all-time list in stolen bases.

For the past few years, Randolph has been the Yankees' third-base coach under Joe Torre. I think Randolph wants to be a manager, and I believe he has all the qualities necessary to be a good one.

**Jerry Coleman**, No. 5 on my all-time Yankees second-baseman list, was as slick a fielder at second as they come, but he wasn't the hitter that Gil McDougald was. Coleman played nine years with the Yankees, had a lifetime batting average of .263, and had only 16 home runs and 217 RBIs in his career. But making the double play, Coleman was as good as they come.

He also missed almost three full seasons while he was serving his country during the Korean War. Coleman flew 120 missions as a marine pilot and was a legitimate war hero, but you'd never know it to talk to him. He never mentioned his exploits.

**Gil McDougald** could make my list of top-five players at three different positions: second base, shortstop, and third base. But because of his versatility, I'm choosing him as the utility player on my all-time Yankees team, which is what he was during his Yankees career.

McDougald played 10 seasons for the Yankees. He played 599 games at second, 508 at third, and 284 at shortstop, and he played each position well enough to have been a regular at any of them. He always batted around .280, .290, would knock in 70 or 80 runs, and hit from 10 to 15 home runs. And he always seemed to make the big play and come up with the clutch hit.

Sad to say that the one thing McDougald will always be remembered for happened one night in Cleveland early in the 1957 season. Herb Score was pitching for the Indians. Let me tell you a little about Score. He was as close to Sandy Koufax as any pitcher I ever saw. As a rookie in 1955, Score won 16 games and led the league in strikeouts with 245. The next year, he won 20 games and led the league with 263 strikeouts and five shutouts. And he was only 23 years old.

His future was unlimited. I have no doubt he would have won 300 games, would have struck out 300 batters in a season several times, and would have pitched a few no-hitters. In other words, Koufax numbers.

But on this night in May 1957, McDougald hit a wicked line drive back to the mound that was hit so hard, Score never saw it. The ball hit him in the head with such force, you could hear the crack all over the stadium. Hearing the sound, and watching Score crumple on the mound, made me sick to my stomach. I thought he was dead.

They took Score to the hospital, and nobody was more upset than McDougald. He couldn't get the sight of Score crumpled on the ground out of his mind, and he threatened to quit the game if anything happened to Score. Fortunately, Score recovered, but he was never the same pitcher.

He played five more seasons and won only 17 more games, no more than 9 in one season. Eventually, he quit baseball and became a broadcaster for the Indians, a job he held for more than 40 years, and he remained one of the good guys and one of the most tragic stories in the history of the game.

McDougald didn't quit baseball, but his career slowly declined, and I often thought that a lot of his decline had to do with what happened to Herb Score. McDougald had batted .311 in 1956 but dropped off 22 points the year of the accident. After that, his average dipped to .250, .251, and .258. He retired after the 1960 season when he was only 32.

# Statistical Summaries

## HITTING

All statistics are for player's Yankees career only.

**G** = Games

**H** = Hits

**HR** = Home runs

**RBI** = Runs batted in

**SB** = Stolen bases

**BA** = Batting average

| Second Baseman | Years | G | H | HR | RBI | SB | BA |
|---|---|---|---|---|---|---|---|
| Tony Lazzeri<br>*First player to hit two grand slams in a game (May 24, 1936)* | 1926–37 | 1,658 | 1,784 | 169 | 1,154 | 147 | .293 |
| Joe Gordon<br>*Most career home runs by an A.L. second baseman (266)* | 1938–43<br>1946 | 1,000 | 1,000 | 153 | 617 | 68 | .271 |
| Bobby Richardson<br>*Set World Series record for most RBIs in a game (6, on October 8, 1960)* | 1955–66 | 1,412 | 1,432 | 34 | 390 | 73 | .266 |

| (continued) | Years | G | H | HR | RBI | SB | BA |
|---|---|---|---|---|---|---|---|
| Willie Randolph<br>*Named to the very first A.L. Silver Slugger team (1980)* | 1976–88 | 1,694 | 1,731 | 48 | 549 | 251 | .275 |
| Jerry Coleman<br>*Led A.L. second basemen in fielding as a rookie (.981 FA)* | 1949–57 | 723 | 558 | 16 | 217 | 22 | .263 |
| Gil McDougald<br>*First rookie to hit a grand slam in the World Series (Game 5, 1951)* | 1951–60 | 1,336 | 1,291 | 112 | 576 | 45 | .276 |

# FIELDING

Statistics are for player's entire career.

**PO** = Put-outs

**A** = Assists

**E** = Errors

**DP** = Double plays

**TC/G** = Total chances divided by games played

**FA** = Fielding average

| Second Baseman | PO | A | E | DP | TC/G | FA |
|---|---|---|---|---|---|---|
| Tony Lazzeri | 3,797 | 5,107 | 341 | 901 | 5.2 | .963 |
| Joe Gordon | 3,826 | 4,726 | 264 | 1,196 | 5.7 | .970 |
| Bobby Richardson | 3,159 | 3,541 | 150 | 977 | 4.9 | .978 |
| Willie Randolph | 4,859 | 6,339 | 237 | 1,547 | 5.3 | .979 |

| (continued) | PO | A | E | DP | TC/G | FA |
|---|---|---|---|---|---|---|
| Jerry Coleman | 1,511 | 1,657 | 89 | 532 | 4.5 | .973 |
| Gil McDougald | 2,352 | 3,373 | 149 | 815 | 4.2 | .975 |

FOUR

# Shortstop

Normally, I wouldn't place a guy No. 1 on my all-time team when he's played only four or five seasons, but the numbers **Derek Jeter** has put up in his short time with the Yankees are mind-boggling and already deserving of the No. 1 ranking among all-time Yankees shortstops.

The difference between Phil Rizzuto (my No. 2 shortstop) and Jeter is anatomical. Rizzuto was listed at 5′6″, and I have my doubts about that. And he weighed 150 pounds soaking wet. Jeter is almost a foot taller at 6′3″, and about a half person heavier at more than 200 pounds. In other words, he's a big man who would have been the biggest player on our 1950 Yankees, an inch taller and several pounds heavier than DiMaggio, and probably would have hit third in our batting order, just in front of Joe D.

1. Derek Jeter

2. Phil Rizzuto

3. Tony Kubek

4. Frank Crosetti

5. Mark Koenig

Size, to me, is the main reason for the upswing in home runs in baseball these days, which is often overlooked when people talk about the power surge. They mention the juiced-up baseball, the smaller stadiums, the inferior pitching, the shrinking strike zone. All those are factors, no doubt. But to me, the biggest reason for the home-run barrage is that players, like all humans, are bigger and stronger than ever.

In his first five seasons with the Yankees, Derek Jeter, my choice as the Yankees' all-time shortstop, put up Hall of Fame numbers and helped the Yankees win four World Series championships.

They lift weights, even before and after games, which was taboo in my day. They use these thin-handled bats and generate so much bat speed that the ball just jumps out of the ballpark. And Derek Jeter is typical of the modern ballplayer.

In his first five seasons, he batted over .300 four times (Rizzuto was over .300 twice in his 13 seasons) and had a career batting average of .322 (49 points higher than Rizzuto's career average). He had more than 200 hits three times in a row, only the third Yankee to do that. The others were Lou

Gehrig and Don Mattingly, putting Jeter in some very select company. Rizzuto had 200 hits in a season once. He hit 200 on the nose in his MVP season, 1950. Jeter hit 24 home runs in 1999. Rizzuto hit only 14 more for his career.

What's more, Jeter did all this and still maintained a high level of play in the field, at least the equal of Rizzuto.

What I like most about Jeter is that he comes to play every day. He plays hard and works hard and is always looking to improve. He never gives up an at-bat and he hits good pitchers. If there's one thing Rizzuto has over Jeter, it's stolen bases. But I believe Jeter could steal a lot more bases than he does if he were on a team that relied more on stealing.

The difference between Derek Jeter and Hall of Famer Phil Rizzuto is some nine inches in height and 50 pounds. Jeter is taller and heavier than any member of the 1950 Yankees, including Joe DiMaggio.

What I said in Chapter Three about it being no coincidence that the Yankees won three American League pennants and two world championships in the first three years after they traded for Willie Randolph also applies to Derek Jeter. In his first five seasons, the Yankees won four American League pennants and four world championships, and that's no coincidence either.

I believe all of the above effectively states the case for Derek Jeter, despite his brief career, as the Yankees' all-time shortstop.

I was spoiled right from the beginning of my career.

I was called up to the Yankees from Kansas City in June of 1950, and in my first start, I had behind me in center field a living legend, Joe DiMaggio. My catcher was Yogi Berra, a future Hall of Famer. I was surrounded by veterans like "Old Reliable" Tommy Henrich, Gene Woodling, Hank Bauer, Billy Johnson, Joe Collins, Jerry Coleman, and Johnny Mize. I was the No. 4 starter behind the Big Three of Allie Reynolds, Vic Raschi, and Eddie Lopat, with veterans Joe Page and Tom Ferrick in the bullpen, and that afforded me the opportunity to break into the major leagues without a great deal of pressure on me to win.

I also had the advantage of having the incomparable "Scooter," **Phil Rizzuto**, at shortstop.

Rizzuto was in his 10th season as the Yankees' shortstop, and 1950 would be his best year. He batted .324, had 200 hits and 36 doubles, scored 125 runs, stole 38 bases, and was voted the American League's Most Valuable Player.

But it was his defense that I appreciated most. He was unbelievable, and it was very reassuring to have him behind me. He made only 14 errors all season, and I can't tell you how many runs he saved for me and how many times he bailed me out with a great play or by starting a double play. The Yankees made 188 double plays that year, and Rizzuto was involved in 123 of them. I won my first nine starts in my rookie season, and I'm not being modest when I say that wouldn't have happened if not for the great defense played behind me.

Rizzuto would stay with the Yankees until August 25, 1956, when he was suddenly and heartlessly released. It happened to be the annual Old-Timers' Day at Yankee Stadium, a day that should have been filled with nostalgia and good fellowship. Instead, there was bitterness when the Yankees announced that Rizzuto was being released. After 13 seasons as a Yankee and all the great years he had given them, you would have thought they would have treated

"The Scooter," Phil Rizzuto, at the height of his Hall of Fame career with the Yankees. He's been associated with the Yankees as a player and broadcaster for almost 60 years.

him with a little more respect. They could have kept him for the remainder of the season, then let him go after the World Series instead of doing it on this of all days.

I know Rizzuto was hurt, and, for a while, he was bitter toward the Yankees.

Here's how it happened. George Weiss, our general manager, had a chance to get the veteran Enos Slaughter from the Kansas City Athletics. Weiss figured Slaughter would be a big help to us, another left-handed bat in Yankee Stadium for the stretch run to the pennant and the World Series. But in order to add Slaughter, Weiss had to make room for him on the roster by dropping a player.

That morning he sent for Rizzuto to come to his office and told him about the Slaughter deal. Then Weiss asked Rizzuto whom he thought the Yankees should drop to make room for Slaughter.

Rizzuto figured because he was a veteran and such a good judge of talent, Weiss was asking his opinion. It turned out that wasn't it at all.

"We could get rid of a pitcher," Scooter told Weiss, who just shook his head no.

"We could send Billy Hunter down to the minor leagues," Rizzuto said.

"No," Weiss said. "I don't think so."

"How about Jerry Lumpe?"

Again, Weiss shook his head. Now Rizzuto was getting the message. Weiss knew what move he wanted to make, and that's why he had called Rizzuto to his office. Finally, Weiss dropped the bomb.

"We have no other choice, Phil," Weiss said. "We've got to release you to make room on our roster for Slaughter."

Rizzuto was crushed. He never expected it. I heard that Rizzuto was in tears when he went down to the clubhouse to clean out his locker. He was hurt, insulted because he felt the Yankees hadn't treated him right after all his years with the team. And it was humiliating to get the news on Old-Timers' Day in front of Joe DiMaggio and all his old teammates.

In 1950, my first year with the Yankees, I watched Phil Rizzuto bat .324, rap out 200 hits, score 125 runs, steal 12 bases, and win the American League's Most Valuable Player award. I also saw him bail me out many times with his brilliant plays at shortstop.

Rizzuto packed his things quickly and left the Stadium before he had to face anybody. He later said if it hadn't been for his old teammate and neighbor George Stirnweiss, who was there for Old-Timers' Day, he didn't know how he would have gotten home. That's how upset he was.

For a while, Rizzuto held a grudge against the Yankees, especially Weiss. He even took a job broadcasting New York Giants games for the rest of the 1956 season.

As it turned out, getting released by the Yankees was a blessing in disguise for Rizzuto. After the season, the Yankees realized they couldn't let Rizzuto get away, especially to the rival Giants. So they offered him a job as a broadcaster, working with Mel Allen and Red Barber. He started broadcasting in 1957 and stayed there for 40 years. That means Rizzuto's association with the Yankees lasted for almost 60 years. Is there anybody else in the history of baseball who was associated with one team that long? I doubt it.

It also means that because he was broadcasting our games, Rizzuto was there for every one of the 18 years I was a Yankees player and coach, and he remains one of my all-time favorite characters.

Rizzuto has this morbid fear of so many things. He was afraid of flying, afraid of lightning, afraid of any kind of crawly bugs or insects. So, naturally, the more he showed his fear, the more we played jokes on him, like putting bugs and insects in the broadcasting booth just to get his reaction.

He also got this reputation for leaving the ballpark early when he was a broadcaster. He'd always find an excuse to get out in the seventh or eighth inning and often boasted he was across the George Washington Bridge and home with his beloved wife, Cora, before the game ended.

But my greatest memory of Rizzuto is what a great shortstop he was. In his 13 seasons, the Yankees won 10 pennants and eight world championships. Ted Williams always said that if his Red Sox had had Rizzuto, they—and not the Yankees—would have won all those pennants.

Rizzuto was typical of the shortstops of his day—small, quick, great defensively—shortstops like Pee Wee Reese in Brooklyn, Johnny Pesky in Boston, Lou Boudreau in Cleveland, Johnny Lipon in Detroit, Alvin Dark with the Giants, and Chico Carrasquel in Chicago. Most of them were there for their gloves, and those that were good hitters were the kind that slapped the ball around, hit behind the runner, bunted—not much power.

Occasionally, a Vern Stephens or an Ernie Banks would come along, and they were big home-run hitters. But they were the exception. Generally, your shortstop was your leadoff or No. 2 hitter.

That's not the case today. In the American League right now, there are three guys playing shortstop who are big enough to be first basemen, third basemen, or outfielders and who hit with enough power to bat third or cleanup for their teams. I'm talking about Alex Rodriguez, Nomar Garciaparra, and Derek Jeter.

It hurts me to say this because of my loyalty to Rizzuto and my respect and affection for him, but I stand by my ranking of Derek Jeter as No. 1 among all-time Yankee shortstops. As much as it pains me, it probably pains Rizzuto more. But if you put a gun to his head (or a caterpillar in his pocket), I believe he would agree with me on this.

*F*or nine consecutive seasons, from 1932 to 1940, Frank Crosetti held down the shortstop position for the New York Yankees and did it skillfully, batting in the .250s and .260s, averaging about 10 home runs and 60 RBIs per year, and playing a defense that was always consistent and often spectacular.

In those nine seasons, the Yankees won five American League pennants and five World Series.

In 1940, at the age of 39, Crosetti began to slide. He batted only .194 and slipped to four home runs and 31 RBIs. The Yankees knew it was time to turn their shortstop job over to someone new.

The Yankees had already handpicked Crosetti's successor. His name was Philip Francis Rizzuto Jr.

Born in Brooklyn, young Rizzuto dreamed of playing for his beloved Brooklyn Dodgers. But he was run out of a Dodgers tryout camp and later endured the same fate at a New York Giants tryout.

"You're too small, kid," he was told. "What makes you think you can play ball? Go home and get yourself a shoeshine box."

He was listed at 5'6" and 150 pounds, but even those meager numbers seemed exaggerations. Nevertheless, the Yankees saw in young Rizzuto what the Dodgers and Giants could not—terrific speed, excellent fielding ability, and, above all, a fierce determination to succeed—and signed him to a contract in 1937 and sent him to Bassett, Virginia, where he batted .310 in 67 games.

He followed that up with better than .300 seasons at Norfolk and Kansas City, the Yankees' top farm team. At Kansas City in 1940, at the age of 22, Rizzuto batted .347 with 10 home runs and 73 RBIs and reported to spring training with the Yankees in 1941 tabbed as their likely starting shortstop.

Said Phil Rizzuto:

*Crosetti was wonderful to me. He was one of the first guys who talked to me. In those days, the veteran players rarely talked to a rookie. But Crow was great. He helped me a lot during spring training. Here I had come to take his job and he was helping me. I couldn't believe it.*

*I opened the season at shortstop, and on opening day we were playing the Washington Senators. I had never seen the Washington Senators before, and Crosetti sat me down and gave me some tips. They had three very good left-handed hitters, Cecil Travis, Buddy Lewis, and Doc Cramer. Although they were left-handed, they hit everything to left field. Crosetti said, "You watch me; I'll position you. I'll move you with every hitter."*

*He had me playing those three left-handed hitters like right-handed hitters, and I made about six or seven plays on them because of Crow positioning me. And I'm trying to take his job. But that's the kind of guy Crow is. He always was everybody's favorite.*

*As a player, he was hard-nosed. He'd stick his hand in the dirt for a ground ball and come up with the ball, dirt and pebbles and all. He could run [a league-leading 27 stolen bases in 1938] and slide, and he had a great arm. He threw straight overhand, and he'd fire rockets to first base. As a hitter, he struck out a lot, but he had great power for a guy his size [5'10", 165 pounds].*

*And smart. He tried to teach me how to get hit by a pitch. He was a master at it. We wore those big, blousy flannel uniforms in those days, and Crow would blossom out his shirt and let the ball hit his shirt without getting him. He'd get on first base a lot that way. He tried to teach me to do the same thing, but I could never do it like him.*

> *When I was broadcasting and we'd go out to play against Oakland,*
> *Frank would come to the games. He lives in Stockton. I'd always say,*
> *"Come on the air with me," but he never would. He was too shy.*
> *When I got into the Hall of Fame, I called him and invited him to*
> *come to Cooperstown. "I'll pay your way," I said. But he said, "I ain't*
> *flying for nobody."*

Once Rizzuto replaced Crosetti as the Yankees' shortstop, except for three years in the navy in World War II, he wouldn't be dislodged for 14 years. After he retired in 1956, Rizzuto remained with the Yankees until the late nineties as a radio and television broadcaster, giving him almost 60 years of continuous service with the team, longer than anyone in Yankees history.

When Rizzuto was released, Gil McDougald took over as our shortstop and played there for two seasons. Then in 1958, along came a young man from Milwaukee named **Tony Kubek**. He was only 22 at the time, and he was our regular shortstop for the next eight years, except for 1962, when he spent most of the season in military service and Tommy Tresh took over and was named Rookie of the Year in the American League.

Tony Kubek is a man of principle. He could have hung around and taken the money, but when he felt he could no longer perform up to his exacting standards, he retired following the 1965 season. He was only 29.

They never played together, but if they had, this would have made an all-star infield (from left): third baseman Red Rolfe, shortstop Frank "Crow" Crosetti, second baseman Gil McDougald, and first baseman Joe Collins.

Kubek had Derek Jeter's size, 6'3", 190 pounds, but he didn't hit for power like Jeter. His high for home runs was 14 in 1960, but he was a consistent left-handed hitter and an exceptional fielder whose greatest contribution was being the shortstop of an American League championship team six times and a World Series championship team three times in his seven seasons as our regular shortstop.

Like his good friend Bobby Richardson, Kubek could have played a few more years and taken the money. But he decided to retire after the 1965 season, at the age of 29. It was typical of Kubek and Richardson that they talked over retiring and decided it would be unfair to the team if both of them retired at the same time. So they made an agreement that they would retire a year apart, Kubek after the 1965 season, Richardson after the 1966 season.

After he retired, Kubek went into broadcasting baseball on television and became one of the best baseball analysts in the business. Again, typical of Tony, he retired at the top of his game.

For No. 4 and No. 5 on my all-time list of Yankees shortstops, I have chosen two players I never saw but have heard a lot about. There's no doubt that **Frank Crosetti** and **Mark Koenig** were there for their defense, and from what I've heard, they played great defense.

*"I had come to take his job and he was helping me. That's the kind of guy Frank Crosetti is. He always was everybody's favorite."*

—PHIL RIZZUTO

Crosetti ("Crow") is another of the Yankees' San Francisco–Italian American connections. He played with the Yankees for 17 years, with a lifetime batting average of .245 and only 98 career home runs. But he was the shortstop on those great teams in the late thirties, playing alongside Tony Lazzeri, Lou Gehrig, and Joe DiMaggio.

When he quit playing, Crosetti was our third-base coach for another 20 years. Managers came and went, but Crosetti in the third-base coach's box was a fixture.

Koenig was the shortstop for the "Murderers Row" Yankees of the late twenties. He played for the Yankees for five seasons and had his best year in 1928 when he batted .319 and drove in 63 runs, his third consecutive year with more than 60 RBIs. In 1930, he was traded to the Detroit Tigers to make room for Lyn Lary at shortstop.

Mark Koenig will be best remembered in baseball history as the man who inspired Babe Ruth's "called shot" home run against the Cubs in the 1932 World Series.

The way the story goes, Koenig, who was a former teammate and a good friend of the Babe, had been picked up by the Cubs from the Tigers in August. He played in only 33 games, but he batted .353 and was believed to be instrumental in putting the Cubs over the top in the National League pennant race. Despite his valuable contributions, without which the Cubs probably would not have won the pennant, Koenig was voted only a half share of the pennant and World Series money by his teammates.

That outraged Ruth, and when the Yankees met the Cubs in the World Series, he kept calling the Cubs cheap bums. The more Ruth ripped the Cubs, the more they ripped him back with insults of their own. They were on Ruth unmercifully, so when he came to bat against Charlie Root in the fifth inning of the third game in Wrigley Field, Ruth took a strike, then pointed toward the right-field seats. He took another strike, then pointed again. Then he hit Root's next pitch right where he had pointed.

Writers in the press box swore that Ruth called his shot. Through the years, Ruth was often asked if he actually called his home run. Sometimes he denied the story, other times he confirmed it. It remains one of the great legends of baseball, but a mystery to this day.

As for Mark Koenig, he was another Yankee from San Francisco. However, he was not an Italian American, proving, I guess, that not all ballplayers who come from San Francisco and wind up playing for the Yankees are Italian Americans.

# Statistical Summaries

## HITTING

All statistics are for player's Yankees career only.

**G** = Games

**H** = Hits

**HR** = Home runs

**RBI** = Runs batted in

**SB** = Stolen bases

**BA** = Batting average

| Shortstop | Years | G | H | HR | RBI | SB | BA |
|---|---|---|---|---|---|---|---|
| Derek Jeter<br>*Third highest BA among active players behind Tony Gwynn and Mike Piazza* | 1995–2000 | 786 | 1,008 | 78 | 414 | 108 | .322 |
| Phil Rizzuto<br>*Expert bunter, led A.L. in sacrifice hits four straight years (1949–52)* | 1941–42<br>1946–56 | 1,661 | 1,588 | 38 | 562 | 149 | .273 |
| Tony Kubek<br>*Homered in final major league at-bat (October 3, 1965)* | 1957–65 | 1,092 | 1,109 | 57 | 373 | 29 | .266 |

| (continued) | Years | G | H | HR | RBI | SB | BA |
|---|---|---|---|---|---|---|---|
| Frank Crosetti<br><br>*Led the A.L. in hit by pitches eight times* | 1932–48 | 1,682 | 1,541 | 98 | 649 | 113 | .245 |
| Mark Koenig<br><br>*Leading batter in the 1927 World Series with nine hits and .500 BA* | 1925–30 | 567 | 636 | 15 | 241 | 11 | .285 |

# FIELDING

Statistics are for player's entire career.

**PO** = Put-outs

**A** = Assists

**E** = Errors

**DP** = Double plays

**TC/G** = Total chances divided by games played

**FA** = Fielding average

| Shortstop | PO | A | E | DP | TC/G | FA |
|---|---|---|---|---|---|---|
| Derek Jeter | 1,198 | 2,062 | 89 | 423 | 4.3 | .973 |
| Phil Rizzuto | 3,220 | 4,666 | 263 | 1,217 | 4.9 | .968 |
| Tony Kubek | 1,808 | 2,850 | 162 | 583 | 4.4 | .966 |
| Frank Crosetti | 3,202 | 4,696 | 421 | 968 | 5.0 | .949 |
| Mark Koenig | 1,987 | 2,929 | 350 | 514 | 4.9 | .934 |

# FIVE

# Third Baseman

ONLY ONE THIRD BASEMAN WHO PLAYED for the Yankees has made the Hall of Fame to date. That was Frank "Home Run" Baker, their third baseman from 1916 until 1922, who had his best years and earned his reputation with the great Philadelphia Athletics of Connie Mack just after the turn of the 20th century. Baker combined with shortstop Jack Barry and second baseman Eddie Collins to form the Athletics' famed "One Hundred Thousand Dollar Infield," when $100,000 was a lot of money.

In seven seasons with the Athletics, Baker batted over .300 five times and over .330 three times. He got his nickname by leading the American League in home runs in four consecutive seasons, from 1911 to 1914. He led the league with 11, 10, 12, and 9 home runs, which tells you how long ago that was. It also tells you that Babe Ruth hadn't arrived on the scene yet.

1. GRAIG NETTLES

2. RED ROLFE

3. CLETE BOYER

4. WADE BOGGS

5. JOE DUGAN

At the top of his game, in 1915, Baker sat out the season in a contract dispute with Connie Mack, the Athletics' manager and owner. Mack found he could not afford the salaries demanded by his championship team, and he began to sell off his players, some of the best in the game. The Yankees purchased Baker for $37,500 on February 15, 1916.

By the time he got to the Yankees, Baker's career was beginning to decline, and sitting out a year didn't help. He batted over .300 just once with the Yankees and had a total of 48 home runs in six seasons. I am therefore reluctant, despite his Hall of Fame career, to place Baker among the top-five Yankees third basemen.

My choice as the Yankees all-time third baseman is **Graig Nettles**. He came from the Cleveland Indians after the 1972 season in a trade for four young players. It was a trade that Ralph Houk, my old manager, wanted very badly. Houk liked Nettles' left-handed power, his defense, and his approach to the game. Nettles had a perfect Yankee Stadium stroke, a left-handed pull hitter who could pop the ball into the short right-field porch. He reminded me a lot of Roger Maris in his swing and his demeanor, except that Nettles was much more outgoing than Maris. Nettles even wore Maris' number 9.

Nettles had come up with the Minnesota Twins under Billy Martin, who had managed him in the minor leagues. He was one of Martin's favorite players, and I could see why.

It was Nettles who instigated the famed controversial "Pine Tar Incident" in 1983. The Yankees were playing the Kansas City Royals, and Nettles noticed that the pine tar on George Brett's bat was too high up on the barrel, above the legal limit. Nettles mentioned it to Martin, who decided he wouldn't say anything to the umpires unless and until Brett got a big hit with the bat.

Sure enough, with two outs in the top of the ninth inning, Brett hit a two-run homer off Goose Gossage that put the Royals ahead 5–4. That's when Martin protested to the umpires and pointed out the pine tar on Brett's bat. The umpires upheld Martin's protest and called Brett out for using an illegal bat, giving the Yankees a 4–3 win.

But the Royals appealed the protest and it went to American League president Lee MacPhail, who overturned the protest. That meant the home run, and the Royals' lead, stayed, and the game would have to be completed at a later date. The Yankees would lose the game, but the "Pine Tar Incident" remains etched in baseball history, and it endeared Nettles to Martin forever.

By then, Nettles had established himself as the Yankees' all-time third baseman by hitting 250 home runs in 11 seasons, the most home runs ever for a Yankees third baseman and the most in American League history for a third baseman. Including his years with Minnesota, Cleveland, San Diego, and

Graig Nettles was an acrobat at third base. His plays against the Dodgers in the 1978 World Series showed the country what New Yorkers had seen for years.

Atlanta, Nettles hit 389 home runs. In 1976, he led the American League in home runs with 32. The following year he hit 37 home runs, the most ever for a Yankees' third baseman, but finished tied for second with Bobby Bonds, two behind Jim Rice.

I got to see Nettles up close when I was the Yankees' pitching coach in 1974 and 1975. We played our home games at Shea Stadium in those two seasons while Yankee Stadium was being renovated, and Nettles had a tough time defensively. With the Mets and Yankees both playing at Shea, the infield was a mess. It was all chewed up from the constant use, and it was rock hard

In the field, Graig Nettles was known for "robbin'" hitters. At the plate, he was "bat man," a dangerous left-handed hitter in Yankee Stadium who led the American League in home runs in 1976.

because it wasn't getting enough water. So the ball took crazy hops on the infield, and Nettles was frustrated because the field was in such terrible shape; it affected his defense and hurt his reputation as a fielder.

That reputation was restored when the Yankees returned to Yankee Stadium in 1976 and in the 1978 World Series against the Dodgers, when Nettles made all those great plays in front of a national television audience.

Nettles also had the reputation, well deserved, as one of the great baseball wits of his time. His sense of humor was sarcastic and biting. Nothing was sacred, not even himself. On his glove, Nettles wrote "E–5," which is the scorer's designation for error, third base.

The other players called Nettles "Puff" because of his ability to disappear in an instant. One minute he was there, and the next minute he was gone. Once when he missed a mandatory team luncheon and was fined, Nettles said, "If they want someone to go to luncheons and make speeches, they can get George Jessel. If they want someone to play third base and hit home runs, they have me."

His most famous line came during all the turmoil of the so-called Bronx Zoo in the late seventies. Commenting on the constant controversy swirling around the Yankees clubhouse almost daily, Nettles said, "Most kids want to grow up and join the circus or play in the major leagues. I'm lucky. I got to do both."

He played 21 years in the major leagues, 11 of them for the Yankees, with enough distinction to be my choice as their all-time third baseman.

*"Most kids want to grow up and join the circus or play in the major leagues. I'm lucky. I got to do both."*

—Graig Nettles

**Robert Abial "Red" Rolfe** was the Yankees third baseman for nine seasons, from 1934 to 1942. He never played for another team. He was a left-handed hitter who had a lifetime batting average of .289. His best season was 1939,

A reunion of Yankees greats at the annual Old-Timers' Day celebration (from left): third baseman Red Rolfe, pitcher Bill Stafford, "The Scooter," Phil Rizzuto, relief ace Johnny Murphy, and "Old Reliable," Tommy Henrich.

when he led the American League with 213 hits, 46 doubles, and 139 runs; batted .329; drove in 80 runs; and hit 14 home runs.

I knew Rolfe as the manager of the Detroit Tigers when I broke in in 1950. He had them in the race right to the end, and we beat them by three games. Rolfe managed the Tigers for two more years, then he left and was the baseball coach at Dartmouth College for many years.

Defensively, **Clete Boyer** was the best third baseman I ever saw in a Yankees uniform. We got him from Kansas City in 1959, and for the next eight seasons, Boyer was a magician at third base. Great hands. Great reflexes. Great arm. He made plays you wouldn't believe. And I appreciated him most, being a left-handed sinkerball pitcher. He bailed me out of many tough spots with his glove.

As a left-handed sinkerball pitcher, I appreciated having a great third baseman like Clete Boyer—the best I've seen, including Brooks Robinson—behind me.

As a hitter, Boyer had trouble with breaking balls and off-speed pitching. His highest average with the Yankees was .272 in 1962, but usually he was in the .240 to .250 range. He had some pop in his bat and twice hit 18 home runs in a season, and he seemed to come up with big hits in big moments.

I remember two of those big moments vividly. In Game 1 of the 1962 World Series in San Francisco, I was locked in a pitching duel with Billy O'Dell of the Giants. After six innings, we were tied, 2–2. Boyer led off the seventh with a home run, and we went on to win the game, 6–2.

*T*he standard by which all third basemen will always be measured is the incomparable Brooks Robinson, the Baltimore Orioles' Minister of Defense, the "human vacuum cleaner." He was the peerless third baseman, simply the best.

He had good career batting statistics—a .267 average, 268 home runs, and 1,357 RBIs—but he batted over .300 just twice, drove in more than 100 runs twice, and never hit more than 28 home runs in his 23 major league seasons, all with the Orioles. So, it's safe to say Brooks Robinson was the first player elected to the Hall of Fame primarily for his defense. Starting in 1960, he won 16 consecutive Gold Gloves, emblematic of defensive excellence at his position and voted upon annually by opposing managers and coaches.

Robinson's defensive skills were never more evident than in the 1970 World Series, won by the Orioles over the Cincinnati Reds in five games. A national television audience was treated to the brilliance of Robinson that American League fans and opponents had witnessed for years.

Robinson excelled at the bat, too, hitting .429 with two home runs and six RBIs in the five games, but it was his defense that dazzled the nation and left the Reds awestruck. Time and time again, he made impossible plays to choke off incipient Reds rallies, darting to his left, flashing to his right, taking away hit after hit from the frustrated, disbelieving Reds.

75

"All I can remember," said Sparky Anderson, then manager of the Reds, "is Brooks Robinson making all those great plays at third base. Every time I looked up, there was Brooksie diving here and diving there to squelch a rally."

For all his brilliance, Robinson always was one of the game's most modest heroes. No self-promoter he, and he was always ready to praise opponents, even other third basemen.

It is for this reason that Brooks Robinson is the perfect man to evaluate his contemporaries—like Isaac Stern critiquing violinists, Luciano Pavarotti judging tenors, Pablo Casals rating cellists.

Said Brooks Robinson:

*I've seen a lot of great third basemen, but none better than Clete Boyer and Graig Nettles. In the sixties, I thought Boyer was the best I ever played against. He was the perfect fit for those Yankees teams. He'd hit an occasional long ball, but he didn't hit for a high average. That team didn't need him to hit. They needed him for his defense, and he was great.*

*It's tough to choose between Boyer and Nettles, that's how close they were in ability. Their styles were different. Boyer had his feet wide apart. Nettles kind of walked into it. Boyer had soft hands and a better arm than Nettles or me.*

*Nettles was good in Minnesota and Cleveland, but he didn't get his due until he went to New York. And then he made all those great plays in the 1978 World Series, and he got the recognition because now you had non–baseball fans watching the games. Everybody was amazed at the plays he made, but the teams he played against knew he had been doing those things all the time.*

*I always thought the World Series of 1970 was my springboard to the Hall of Fame. I played 23 years, and I never had five games in a row like that.*

*The great defensive third basemen in my time were Boyer, Nettles, Mike Schmidt, Sal Bando, Buddy Bell. Aurelio Rodriguez was as good as anybody, and he had the best arm I ever saw on a third baseman. But you have to put up some offensive numbers to get noticed.*

> *Who's the best? It depends on who you talk to. If you talk to Tim McCarver, he'll say Mike Schmidt. If you talk to Larry King, he'll say Billy Cox.*
>
> *Cox played for the Brooklyn Dodgers in the fifties, before I came along, and everybody who saw him tells me what a great third baseman he was. In Baltimore, our public address announcer was Rex Barney, who pitched for the Dodgers, and he used to kid me all the time about Billy Cox. If I made a good play, Rex would tell me, "Billy Cox would have made it easier." If I didn't come up with a ball, Rex would say, "Billy Cox would have had it."*
>
> *Funny thing, Billy Cox ended his career in Baltimore in 1955, the year I came up. But I got there on June 1, and he had just been released, so I never got to see him. I wish I had because I heard so much about him.*

In the 1964 World Series, it came down to the seventh game between us and the Cardinals. We went into the ninth inning down 7–3, when Boyer hit a home run. But we lost the game, 7–5, and the Series. Clete's brother Ken hit a home run for the Cardinals in the same game.

But it was Boyer's defense that made him so valuable. Fortunately, those Yankees teams in the sixties had so much offensive fire power, we could live with a defensive specialist such as Boyer at a power position. As a pitcher, I know how critical our great infield defense was to winning all those pennants.

Clete was the youngest of three brothers to play in the major leagues. His oldest brother, Cloyd, was a journeyman pitcher for the St. Louis Cardinals and Kansas City Royals. His brother Ken was an all-star third baseman for the Cardinals who had five seasons over .300 and seven seasons with 24 or more home runs; he led the National League in RBIs in 1964 with 119. But Ken wasn't the fielder Clete was.

I feel certain that if you could take Clete Boyer's glove and Ken Boyer's bat and combine them into one player, you'd have a Hall of Famer and the No. 1 third baseman in Yankees history.

**Wade Boggs** was one of the truly great pure hitters of all-time. He had a lifetime batting average over .330, had more than 3,000 hits, won five batting titles, and had 200 hits in a season seven times. He'll be elected to the Hall of Fame as soon as he's eligible, and he may even choose a Yankees cap for his Hall of Fame plaque, but he is most closely associated with the Boston Red Sox, with whom he had most of his 3,000 hits, all five of his batting titles, and all seven of his 200-hit seasons.

Boggs signed with the Yankees as a free agent before the 1993 season and played six seasons in New York. He batted over .300 in his first five years (he was under .300 just once in his first fifteen seasons), but it was clear he was no longer the hitter he once was. In his final season with the Yankees, 1997, Boggs had 103 hits and batted .292. He was 39 at the time.

Had he played his entire career with the Yankees, future Hall of Famer Wade Boggs would be my choice as their all-time third baseman. In his five seasons as a Yankee, Boggs batted over .300 four times, including a .342 average in 1994 at the age of 36. *Photo used by permission of Chuck Solomon/TimePix.*

Like Frank Baker and Wade Boggs, **"Jumping" Joe Dugan** came from another team and had a brief career with the Yankees. Dugan had replaced "Home Run" Baker as the Athletics' third baseman, then he was traded to the Boston Red Sox before the 1922 season in a three-team deal involving Boston, Philadelphia, and Washington. Interestingly, in the deal, the Washington Senators got former Yankees shortstop Roger Peckinpaugh.

Midway through the 1922 season, the Yankees obtained Dugan and outfielder Elmer Smith from the Red Sox for $50,000 and four players, including Lefty O'Doul, another of the Yankees' San Francisco connections—although not an Italian—who would become one of Joe DiMaggio's closest friends.

Dugan was the third baseman for the Yankees famed "Murderers Row" of Ruth, Gehrig, and Lazzeri. He had six and a half seasons with the Yankees and was a consistent .280 to .300 hitter, but he hit only 22 home runs in a Yankees uniform and never drove in more than 67 runs in any one season.

How's this for a coincidence? When I was a kid in Astoria, there was an older man who hung around the sandlots quite a bit. He was kind of an unofficial baseball coach for all the kids in the neighborhood. He would teach us how to field and hit properly. He was very knowledgeable about the game and well respected in the neighborhood because of his knowledge. He helped a lot of kids improve.

The man's name was Dugan, and it was well known in the neighborhood that he was the brother of "Jumping" Joe Dugan, who played for the Yankees. I didn't even know who "Jumping" Joe Dugan was, but we all thought it was pretty cool to have the brother of a former Yankee teaching us the fine points of the game.

# Statistical Summaries

## HITTING

All statistics are for player's Yankees career only.

**G** = Games

**H** = Hits

**HR** = Home runs

**RBI** = Runs batted in

**SB** = Stolen bases

**BA** = Batting average

| Third Baseman | Years | G | H | HR | RBI | SB | BA |
|---|---|---|---|---|---|---|---|
| Graig Nettles<br>*Most career home runs by an A.L. third baseman (319)* | 1973–83 | 1,535 | 1,396 | 250 | 834 | 18 | .253 |
| Red Rolfe<br>*Scored over 100 runs for seven consecutive seasons (1935–41)* | 1931<br>1934–42 | 1,175 | 1,394 | 69 | 497 | 44 | .289 |
| Clete Boyer<br>*Led A.L. in fielding chances per game five consecutive seasons (1961–65)* | 1959–66 | 1,068 | 882 | 95 | 393 | 27 | .241 |

| (continued) | Years | G | H | HR | RBI | SB | BA |
|---|---|---|---|---|---|---|---|
| **Wade Boggs** <br> *Won two Gold Glove Awards as a Yankee (1994, 1995)* | 1993–97 | 602 | 702 | 24 | 246 | 4 | .313 |
| **Joe Dugan** <br> *Had four hits in Game 5 of 1923 World Series (Yanks 8, Giants 1)* | 1922–28 | 785 | 871 | 22 | 320 | 12 | .286 |

## FIELDING

Statistics are for player's entire career.

**PO** = Put-outs

**A** = Assists

**E** = Errors

**DP** = Double plays

**TC/G** = Total chances divided by games played

**FA** = Fielding average

| Third Baseman | PO | A | E | DP | TC/G | FA |
|---|---|---|---|---|---|---|
| Graig Nettles | 2,098 | 5,315 | 298 | 480 | 3.1 | .961 |
| Red Rolfe | 1,336 | 2,275 | 170 | 216 | 3.3 | .955 |
| Clete Boyer | 1,902 | 3,810 | 198 | 443 | 3.5 | .966 |
| Wade Boggs | 2,113 | 4,305 | 232 | 471 | 2.1 | .965 |
| Joe Dugan | 1,905 | 3,016 | 277 | 338 | 3.7 | .947 |

# SIX

# Left Fielder

You could make the argument, and some have, that **Dave Winfield** is the greatest athlete ever to play major league baseball. I emphasize the word *athlete*. When he graduated from the University of Minnesota, Winfield was drafted in the three major sports—baseball, basketball, and football. He chose baseball and signed with the San Diego Padres. He never spent a day in the minor leagues.

Winfield stands 6'6" tall and weighs 220 pounds, and he could do it all— run, hit, hit for power, field, and throw. He was what major league scouts call a "five-tool player."

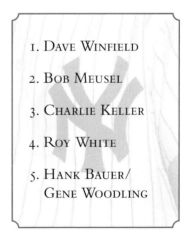

1. Dave Winfield

2. Bob Meusel

3. Charlie Keller

4. Roy White

5. Hank Bauer/ Gene Woodling

After 8 years with the Padres, Winfield signed as a free agent with the Yankees for 10 years at the then unheard of and staggering sum of $15 million.

Winfield's 10 years with the Yankees were filled with great deeds on the field and controversy off the field. In his first season with the Yankees, 1981, they won the American League pennant but lost to the Dodgers in the World Series, four games to two. Winfield had a horrible Series against the Dodgers, just one hit in 22 at-bats, and George Steinbrenner publicly criticized his new superstar, calling him "Mr. May," a reference to Winfield playing well early in the season but failing in the big games. To further irritate Winfield, the "Mr. May" reference was an implied comparison with Steinbrenner's previous superstar, Reggie Jackson, whose performances in the World Series earned him the nickname, "Mr. October."

Winfield had some great seasons with the Yankees. Once he batted .340, another time .322. Six times in his first eight seasons in New York, he had more than 20 homers. Six times he drove in 100 or more runs.

Dave Winfield was drafted in three major sports—baseball, football, and basketball. He chose baseball and signed with the San Diego Padres without ever having played a game in the minor leagues. He came to the Yankees in 1981 and proceeded to earn my selection as the team's No. 1 all-time left fielder. He's the latest former Yankee elected to the Hall of Fame, a much-deserved honor.

At 6'6" tall, Dave Winfield was an intimidating figure at the plate. But he was not a player who could be intimidated by pitchers throwing at him, which they often did.

But the Yankees never won a World Series championship in Winfield's years with them, and that added to the rift between him and Steinbrenner. Later, there were charges by Steinbrenner that Winfield was misusing contributions from Steinbrenner intended for Winfield's foundation. It got to be an ugly scene, and when Winfield missed the entire 1989 season because of back surgery, Steinbrenner had had it with his big man. In May of 1990, Winfield was traded to the California Angels for pitcher Mike Witt.

To his credit, Winfield shook the "loser" label he acquired in New York and got his World Series ring with the Toronto Blue Jays. He would finish his career with more than 3,000 hits, 400 home runs, and 1,500 RBIs. And I'm happy to say that after not returning to Yankee Stadium for several years, Winfield has since buried the hatchet with Steinbrenner and has been back for Old-Timers' Days.

Winfield was elected to the Hall of Fame in 2001, his first year of eligibility (entering as a Padre). Except for Babe Ruth and Joe DiMaggio, who played a handful of games in left field early in their Yankees careers, and Enos Slaughter, whose best years were with the St. Louis Cardinals, he is the first Yankees left fielder to make the Hall of Fame.

86

Another of those players I never saw play is **Bob Meusel**, the left fielder for the Yankees during the entire decade of the twenties. He was a big man for his day, 6′3″, 190 pounds. He played 11 seasons, 10 with the Yankees and 1 with Cincinnati, and had a lifetime batting average of .309.

How good was Meusel? In the early part of his career, he batted fourth for the Yankees, behind Babe Ruth and in front of Lou Gehrig. When Gehrig began to establish himself as an RBI machine, Meusel was dropped to fifth in the batting order.

In the nine-year period from 1923 through 1931, Ruth led the American League in home runs eight times. The one time he did not lead the league in homers, Meusel did. That was in 1925, the year of Ruth's famous "bellyache." He played in only 98 games and hit 25 homers. Meusel led the American League with 33 homers and 138 RBIs.

I got to the Yankees one year after **Charlie Keller** left and went to Detroit. He had been a Yankee every year from 1939 until 1949, except for time out in military service during World War II, and was part of one of the greatest outfields of all-time—Joe DiMaggio, Tommy Henrich, and Keller.

From 1923 through 1931, Babe Ruth led the American League in home runs every year but one. The one year he didn't, 1925, this man did. He's Bob Meusel, the left fielder on the famed and feared "Murderers Row" Yankees of the twenties. *Photo courtesy of the Baseball Hall of Fame.*

The fans and writers called him "King Kong" Keller after the famous movie ape that climbed the Empire State Building. Keller got the nickname because he was stocky and very muscular, and he gave off the image of brute strength, although he was only 5'10" and weighed only 185 pounds. But he could hit and hit with power.

*O*utfielder Tommy Henrich on Charlie Keller:

*For his hitting, I'd have to rate Charlie Keller as the best left fielder I ever played with on the Yankees. He wasn't the best outfielder you ever laid eyes on, but, then, neither was I. He was better than average as a fielder, he didn't have the best arm I ever saw, and he wasn't the fastest guy, but he was smart, and he applied himself. Whatever abilities he had, he got the most out of them.*

*Let me say this about Charlie. He was one of my favorite people. All man. If Charlie told you something, you could go to the bank with it. I had total respect for Charlie. He was as decent a man as I have ever known. I admire him so much.*

*Charlie was quiet, but he could be outspoken when he had to be. About 10 years ago, someone asked him who was the best left-handed pitcher the Yankees ever had, and Charlie said, "Without question, you have to give it to Whitey Ford." And that's a true statement.*

*It was his ability as a hitter that made Charlie such a great ballplayer. You look at his record and see all the home runs he hit [30 or more in a season three times], and you figure it was because of the short right-field porch in Yankee Stadium. The Yankees wanted him to be a pull hitter to take advantage of that short porch, but Charlie wasn't a natural pull hitter, so the short porch didn't help him that much.*

*The ball went where it was pitched. If they pitched him away, he'd hit it to left field and in the gap in left-center. I remember him telling me once in his later years, "If [Joe] McCarthy hadn't made me into a pull hitter, I could have added 20 points to my average."*

*One year, the Yankees sent me down to Newark for 10 days. When I got there, the season was about three weeks old and Charlie was batting about .500. In the 10 days I was there, all he did was hit line drives. They couldn't get him out. He was awesome.*

*People who never saw him—and because of his nickname, "King Kong" Keller—thought Charlie was a big guy. But he wasn't. I was taller than him [Henrich, 6'0"; Keller, 5'10"]. But what a frame he had. Thick and muscular through the chest and shoulders, which is where his power came from.*

*Lefty Gomez gave him that name, "King Kong." It was about the time the movie with Fay Wray came out, and Gomez pinned the name on Charlie, I guess, because he was built like an ape. Plus the K in his last name, it kind of sounded nice together, and the writers picked up on it and it stuck.*

*I loved Lefty, but that was one thing I wish he hadn't done because Charlie didn't like the nickname. It kind of put him down and embarrassed him.*

*Charlie never liked the attention. For that reason, he never was very comfortable in New York. Oh, he liked playing there, but to him it was just a job. He was a country boy, and he was happier being back home in Maryland, raising his horses.*

Phil Rizzuto on Keller:

*My rookie year, the veterans were always playing practical jokes on me. Not just me. They used to play practical jokes on all rookies back then.*

*Charlie Keller was the left fielder, and he was a real quiet guy. They started calling him "King Kong" Keller, and one of the veterans told me, "If you want to get in good with Charlie, call him 'King Kong.' He loves that."*

*So one day I was in the clubhouse and Charlie passed and I called him "King Kong." Oh boy, did he get mad. He picked me up and dropped me in a wastebasket. I was lucky he didn't take a swing at me. He would have killed me. From that day, I never called him "King Kong" again.*

Three times in his Yankees career Keller hit 30 or more home runs. Three times he drove in more than 100 runs. And twice he batted over .300. Keller came back to the Yankees in 1952. He appeared in two games, batted once and struck out, then retired. He had a bad back, and he wanted to get into his first love, harness racing.

*"If Charlie told you something, you could go to the bank with it."* —Tommy Henrich

Keller became a legend in harness racing and a very wealthy man by breeding and racing harness horses. I didn't know him very well when he played baseball, but we got to be good friends after he retired from baseball through our mutual friend, the Hall of Fame harness driver and trainer Del Miller.

90

One of the classiest, most popular, and most unappreciated Yankees of all time was the "Quiet Man," **Roy White**. We were teammates in 1965, 1966, and 1967, the end of my career and the beginning of his. And he was with the team when I coached the Yankees in 1974 and 1975.

White was a professional through and through. He kept his mouth shut, worked hard, caused no problems, and did his job. And he did it well. A switch-hitter, he could run and hit for occasional power despite his size, 5'10", 160 pounds. For example, he had 22 homers, 109 RBIs, and a .296 average in 1970.

Unfortunately, White's best years came when the team was in its 12-year drought. He was an ideal No. 2 hitter in the lineup, but because the Yankees lacked a legitimate power hitter, White had to bat fourth most of the time in the late sixties and early seventies.

When the team started to improve under George Steinbrenner's ownership with players like Chris Chambliss, Graig Nettles, Thurman Munson, and Reggie Jackson, White was moved into the No. 2 slot in the lineup and was a fixture there, and in left field, on the championship teams in 1976, 1977, and 1978. White ended up with an outstanding 15-year career, all with one team.

Roy White (left), who by 1984 was a coach with the Yanks, with Phil Niekro.

**Hank Bauer** and **Gene Woodling**. Gene Woodling and Hank Bauer.

It's almost impossible for me to think of one without thinking of the other. They were like a two-headed monster, 1 and 1A. Their names were practically inseparable. Bauer and Woodling. Hank Woodling. Gene Bauer.

Bauer and Woodling both were there, solidly entrenched in the Yankees outfield, when I came in 1950. Many times they played in the same outfield, usually Bauer in right and Woodling in left, but there also were many times when they were interchangeable.

One of the reasons Casey Stengel earned his reputation as a great manager was his use of the platoon system: right-handed hitters against left-handed pitchers, left-handed hitters against right-handed pitchers.

Switch-hitter Roy White and I were teammates for three seasons at the end of my career and the beginning of his. He was one of the few bright spots for the Yankees during their down period in the late sixties and early seventies.

Stengel wasn't the first manager to platoon players. Managers always platooned, but not to the degree Stengel did. He popularized it and had great success with it, and Woodling and Bauer became the symbols of Stengel's platoon system, often alternating at one outfield position depending on the opposing pitcher. Woodling, a left-handed hitter, would start against right-handed pitchers. Bauer, a right-handed hitter, started against lefties.

Hank Bauer looked like what he was—a tough marine. He was a decorated World War II hero and a good guy to have on your side in a tough ballgame or a fight. *Photo courtesy of the Baseball Hall of Fame.*

Neither of them liked it very much. Both believed they were good enough to play every day, against all kinds of pitching, and their records prove they were. On any other team, or with any other manager, they would have been regulars against all types of pitching. But you have to say the system worked.

Stengel used to say, "They complain about it, but they go to the bank every winter." What he meant was that playing as a righty-lefty platoon, Bauer and Woodling cashed a World Series check every year. Both were members of, and important contributors to, the Yankees' five consecutive world championship teams from 1949 through 1953.

Bauer came to the Yankees in 1948. He had been a decorated marine hero in World War II, and his reputation as a tough marine followed him into baseball. On the field, Bauer was as tough as he looked. He played hard and he played to win. And it was nice to know he was there on your side if a fight broke out. Off the field, Bauer was, and is, a pussycat.

He played 12 seasons with the Yankees, then was involved in the trade that brought Roger Maris to the team. Bauer finished up his career with two seasons in Kansas City. He had a career batting average of .277 with 164 home runs and 703 RBIs.

In 1961, Bauer was named manager of the Kansas City Athletics. After finishing ninth in 1962, he was fired, and in 1963 he took a job as a coach with the Baltimore Orioles under manager Billy Hitchcock.

We had a weekend series in Baltimore early that season. Mickey Mantle had some friends from Dallas who had just bought a farm outside of Baltimore; they invited him for dinner, and he asked me to go along with him.

There was dinner, then drinks after dinner. A lot of drinks. Because I had pitched that day and Mantle was on the disabled list, abstinence was not a requirement. But we still both had to be at the ballpark in time for the next day's game.

The next thing you knew, Mantle and I both fell asleep on the porch. When we woke up, it was dawn, and we had to hustle to get to the ballpark on time. We didn't even bother going back to our hotel. We went straight to the stadium.

When we got there, I got Mantle into the shower, then into the whirlpool, then I let him fall asleep on the trainer's table until it was time for batting practice.

Bauer took one look at Mantle trying to hit in BP, and he knew immediately that we had been out late the night before.

"You look awful," Bauer said to Mantle.

"It's all right," said Mantle. "I'm not playing today. I'm on the disabled list."

When the game started, Mantle and I sat down on the bench, as far away from Ralph Houk as we could get. Mantle put on sunglasses and kept dozing off in the dugout.

Mike McCormick, a veteran left-hander, was pitching a terrific game for the Orioles, and he took a lead going into the ninth inning. Just as the inning started, I noticed Houk get up and start walking down to our end of the bench. I jabbed Mantle in the ribs with my elbow.

"Wake up, Mick," I said. "Houk's coming."

Houk came right up to Mantle and asked, "Can you hit?"

"I'm not eligible," Mantle said. "I'm on the disabled list."

"No you're not," said Houk. "You were activated today."

Mantle was in a spot. He couldn't tell Houk he was hungover, so he reached for his cap, which I had been sitting on. Mantle put the rumpled hat on his head, then headed for the bat rack.

"Just swing at the first pitch you see," I told him.

As Mantle kneeled in the on-deck circle, I could see Bauer saying something to Hitchcock. Then when Mantle was announced as a pinch-hitter, Bauer went to the mound to talk to McCormick.

Later, Bauer said he told McCormick, "This guy's hungover. Don't throw him a strike. He can't see the ball."

McCormick's first pitch was head high, and Mantle, following my advice, swung at it and hit it over the fence. As he rounded the bases, there was Bauer standing on the top step of the Orioles' dugout cursing at Mantle.

When he got back to the bench, Mantle plopped down next to me.

"Hitting the ball was easy," he said. "Running around the bases was the tough part."

Bauer eventually replaced Hitchcock as manager of the Orioles in 1964. He managed the Orioles for five years, then later managed the Oakland Athletics for one year. He won a pennant with the Orioles in 1966, my next to last season with the Yankees, and I figured if we couldn't win the pennant (we finished last), I was rooting for my buddy Bauer to win it. Then he pulled off one of the biggest upsets in World Series history when he swept the Dodgers, with Sandy Koufax and Don Drysdale, in four games. So, as a World Series manager, Bauer was a perfect 1.000. Four games, four wins.

A year after Bauer arrived in New York, the Yankees bought Gene Woodling from the Pittsburgh Pirates. Woodling was one of those pure hitters with a batting style that was reminiscent of Stan Musial, in a crouch and curled up like a corkscrew. But he could hit. In six seasons with the Yankees, he batted over .300 twice.

The one thing I remember most about Woodling is that he always killed Cleveland. Even with their big four of Bob Feller, Bob Lemon, Early Wynn, and Mike Garcia, they couldn't get him out, and that was especially frustrating for the Indians because Woodling came up to the major league with them and was from nearby Akron, Ohio.

Woodling would go on to play for five more teams in a 17-year career with a lifetime batting average of .284. He finished up his career in 1962, playing for Casey Stengel and the original New York Mets. He batted .274 in 81 games for the Mets. He was 40 years old at the time.

# Statistical Summaries

## HITTING

All statistics are for player's Yankees career only.

**G** = Games

**H** = Hits

**HR** = Home runs

**RBI** = Runs batted in

**SB** = Stolen bases

**BA** = Batting average

| Left Fielder | Years | G | H | HR | RBI | SB | BA |
|---|---|---|---|---|---|---|---|
| Dave Winfield<br><br>*Collected a hit in seven consecutive All-Star Games (1982–88)* | 1981–88<br>1990 | 1,172 | 1,300 | 205 | 818 | 76 | .290 |
| Bob Meusel<br><br>*Hit for the cycle a record three times (May 7, 1921; July 3, 1922; July 26, 1928)* | 1920–29 | 1,294 | 1,565 | 146 | 1,005 | 131 | .311 |
| Charlie Keller<br><br>*Batted .438 in 1939 World Series vs. Reds with three homers in four games* | 1939–43<br>1945–49<br>1952 | 1,066 | 1,053 | 184 | 723 | 45 | .286 |

| (continued) | Years | G | H | HR | RBI | SB | BA |
|---|---|---|---|---|---|---|---|
| Roy White<br><br>*Switch-hitter, hit 118 of his 160 home runs left-handed* | 1965–79 | 1,881 | 1,803 | 160 | 758 | 233 | .271 |
| Hank Bauer<br><br>*Hit safely in record 17 consecutive World Series games (1956–58)* | 1948–59 | 1,406 | 1,326 | 158 | 654 | 48 | .277 |
| Gene Woodling<br><br>*Career batting average of .318 in 26 World Series games* | 1949–54 | 698 | 648 | 51 | 336 | 13 | .285 |

# FIELDING

Statistics are for player's entire career.

**PO** = Put-outs

**A** = Assists

**E** = Errors

**DP** = Double plays

**TC/G** = Total chances divided by games played

**FA** = Fielding average

| Left Fielder | PO | A | E | DP | TC/G | FA |
|---|---|---|---|---|---|---|
| Dave Winfield | 5,012 | 168 | 95 | 38 | 1.8 | .982 |
| Bob Meusel | 2,494 | 278 | 129 | 52 | 2.1 | .956 |
| Charlie Keller | 2,235 | 46 | 46 | 6 | 2.3 | .980 |
| Roy White | 3,443 | 122 | 52 | 19 | 2.1 | .986 |

| (continued) | PO | A | E | DP | TC/G | FA |
|---|---|---|---|---|---|---|
| Hank Bauer | 2,384 | 107 | 46 | 20 | 1.7 | .982 |
| Gene Woodling | 2,924 | 93 | 35 | 13 | 1.9 | .989 |

## SEVEN

# Center Fielder

I HAVE A DILEMMA. WHO IS the Yankees' greatest center fielder? My heart says Mickey Mantle, my buddy, my teammate, my running mate. He was the brother I never had.

But my head says **Joe DiMaggio**.

How can you ignore the .325 lifetime batting average, the two batting titles, the two home-run championships, the two RBI titles? How can you discount the 56-game hitting streak? It's a record I feel safe in saying will never be broken—at least not in my lifetime.

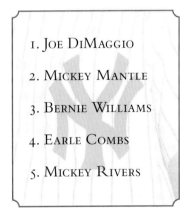

1. JOE DIMAGGIO

2. MICKEY MANTLE

3. BERNIE WILLIAMS

4. EARLE COMBS

5. MICKEY RIVERS

There's also what I consider DiMag's greatest accomplishment and his most unbelievable statistic—only 369 strikeouts in a 13-year career covering 6,829 at-bats. Hell, Mantle had 371 strikeouts in three seasons, 1958 through 1960. In 1941, when he hit in those 56 consecutive games, DiMaggio struck out only 13 times in 541 at-bats.

As a kid growing up in Astoria, Queens, I was always a Yankees fan, and the main reason was DiMaggio. I idolized him. I remember every morning

I consider myself blessed to have pitched all of my 16 seasons in the major leagues with legendary center fielders behind me—first Joe DiMaggio (left), then Mickey Mantle.

my father would buy the *New York Daily News* for two cents, and the first thing I would do when he brought the paper home was turn to the sports section and look at the box score to see how many hits DiMaggio got the day before.

In school, we used to have this betting pool where you would pick three players for a penny, and if your three players got six hits among them, you would get back 6-to-1 odds. I would always pick Joe DiMaggio and Ted Williams and one other player. It was a sucker bet because it's hard to pick three players who would get six hits, even with DiMaggio and Williams—especially Williams because he walked so much, he sometimes would get only two at-bats in a game.

The best time for me when I was a kid was when my uncles would take me up to Yankee Stadium. For a nickel, we'd ride the subway from Astoria all the way up to the Bronx, which took about an hour. We'd sit in the bleachers, where tickets cost 25 cents. So for 35 cents for the ticket and round-trip subway fare, and maybe another 25 cents for a hot dog and a Coke, I'd get to see my idol, the great DiMaggio, in person.

Imagine how I felt when, only 10 years later, I was on the pitcher's mound at Yankee Stadium pitching for my favorite team, and my idol was behind me in center field.

I'll never forget the first time I saw DiMag up close. It was the spring of 1950. I had been invited to spring training in St. Petersburg after going 16–5 in Binghamton the previous season. I boarded a train at Grand Central Station for the 24-hour trip to Florida and checked into the Soreno Hotel.

The next day, I reported to Miller Huggins Field and walked into the clubhouse for the first time. There were about 50 guys crowded into this one little room. I was scared to death just being there, too scared to even talk to anybody. I looked around and I could see some familiar faces, veteran players like Tommy Henrich, Johnny Lindell, Cliff Mapes, Gene Woodling, and Ralph Houk. I recognized Yogi Berra, or Larry Berra, as he was introduced to me the day I signed with the Yankees. And I recognized Charlie Silvera because I had played against him in Mexico.

Pete Sheehy, the clubhouse man, had all the veteran players on one side of the room, and you could tell how much status each player had by the size of his locker and where it was placed. All the rookies were in the back. That's when I met Billy Martin for the first time, but I can't remember anything special that he said or did.

I was in the clubhouse about 15 minutes when the door flew open and in walked Joe DiMaggio, my idol, all dressed up in a suit and tie. I had never seen a suit that good in my life. He looked so dapper, and when he walked through the door, it was like a senator or an ambassador entering a room. I'm sure I remained with my mouth wide open staring at him. I kept sneaking peeks at him, and if DiMaggio happened to turn and look in my direction, I'd turn away so he wouldn't catch me staring at him.

The first thing DiMaggio did when he came in every morning was yell out to Pete Sheehy, "Half a cup of coffee, Petey boy."

And Sheehy would bring him his coffee, and DiMaggio would sit in front of his locker, sipping his coffee and talking with veteran players like Lindell, Mapes, Henrich, and Joe Page. I never saw him talking to any rookies, except Billy Martin, and that was because Martin started the conversation. Martin was so outgoing that by the time spring training was over, he was not only talking to Joe like he was DiMag's equal, he was hanging out with him.

I don't think I said a word to DiMaggio all spring. I was so nervous, I wasn't about to go over to him and introduce myself. I was afraid if I did, I'd get so tongue-tied I was liable to forget my own name.

When spring training was over, I was sent down to Kansas City, where I stayed until July. Then I came up to the Yankees, and there I was, pitching for them with DiMaggio behind me in center field.

By the time I came up, DiMaggio was at the end of his career, and he was hurting because of a bone spur on his heel. He was not the same player he had been, but he was still pretty good. He couldn't run like he used to, but he got such a great jump on the ball in center field that he was still a graceful and excellent outfielder.

When I joined the team, DiMaggio was hitting about .235, but he ended up hitting .301 for the season, so he must have batted about .370 in the time I was there. He was still so graceful in the field and such a good hitter, it made me realize how great he must have been in his prime.

We won the pennant in 1950 and swept the Phillies in the World Series in four games. DiMaggio homered in the tenth inning of the second game to give us a 2–1 win. I started the fourth game, and Joe doubled in a run in the first. We won the game, 5–2, and took the Series.

DiMaggio batted .308 for the Series, and that would be the last time I played with him. I spent 1951 and 1952 in the army, and Joe retired after the 1951 season.

When you're a Yankee, you often find yourself in the company of greatness. Here I am (left) alongside three baseball legends: "The Scooter," "The Mick," and "The Clipper"—Phil Rizzuto, Mickey Mantle, and Joe DiMaggio.

It would be unfair for me to compare DiMaggio and **Mantle** from my personal experience because I played with DiMaggio just that one season, and I played with Mantle for my entire career. Based on my experience, there's no doubt that Mantle was the greatest player I ever saw.

I went into the army soon after the 1950 World Series, so I was not there in spring training in 1951 when Mantle made such an impression on Stengel, the writers, the fans, his teammates, everybody. The Yankees and Giants had traded training sites that spring. The Giants took the Yankees' camp in St. Petersburg, and the Yanks went to Phoenix and used the Giants' training field.

From what I heard and read in the newspapers, Mantle put on quite a display of power in batting practice that entire spring. He hit balls to places that had never been reached before, and not all of it was because of the light Arizona air.

Stengel was so excited by his new boy, he brought Mantle to New York with the team even though Mick was just 19 years old and had played only two seasons in the low minor leagues. Stengel saw in Mantle the successor to DiMaggio, who was winding down his career.

A young Mickey Mantle (left) and the man he replaced in center field for the Yankees, the incomparable Joe DiMaggio.

Unfortunately, Mantle struggled in his first few months with the Yankees. He struck out a lot, and Stengel decided it was best that Mantle go down to Kansas City to work on some things and regain his confidence. But Mantle was so discouraged, he called his father in Oklahoma and said he was thinking of quitting baseball.

Mutt Mantle, who had taught Mickey to switch-hit when he was little and who had spent his entire life working in the mines, drove to Kansas City. Mickey expected his dad to talk him out of quitting. Instead, Mutt took another tack.

"If that's all the guts you have that you can't take it when the going is rough," Mutt said, "then pack your bags and come on home with me."

Mick was stunned. And because of his father's attitude, he realized he would be just a quitter if he went home. He decided to stay. He was back with the Yankees after a few weeks in Kansas City. He finished out his rookie season batting .267 with 13 homers and 65 RBIs in 96 games. Then in the first game of the 1951 World Series against the New York Giants, Mantle stepped on a drainage ditch going after a fly ball in right field and tore up his knee. That injury would plague him for the rest of his career.

DiMaggio retired after the 1951 World Series and Mantle took over DiMaggio's center-field position in 1952. He batted .311 with 23 homers and 87 RBIs, and I got to witness firsthand the enormous power of Mantle that I had heard so much about. I couldn't believe how good he was, how fast he ran, how much power he had.

I caught my first real glimpse of the legendary Mantle batting power in April of 1953. We were playing the Washington Senators in Griffith Stadium, and, batting right-handed, Mantle got into a pitch from Chuck Stobbs and hit it clear over the bleachers. Red Patterson, our publicity director, supposedly found a tape measure and marked off the distance and reported it as 565 feet, the longest home run in Griffith Stadium history. It was with that home run, and Patterson's measurement, that the term "tape measure home run" came into the language of baseball.

By the time I was discharged from the army and rejoined the Yankees in the spring of 1953, Mantle was a full-fledged star and a changed man.

I remembered when he was a minor leaguer and he and Moose Skowron traveled with us during the 1950 season—a kid of 18, very shy, wearing overalls, plaid shirts, and canvas shoes. A typical Oklahoma hick. We never even spoke to one another. The first time I met him was at my wedding.

Joan and I got married on April 14, 1951, while I was on leave from the army. The reception was in Donahue's bar in Astoria, a nice place on Steinway Street with an upstairs room that seated about 150 people.

As a courtesy, Joan's mother sent an invitation to Red Patterson, the Yankees' public relations director. We never expected anybody to show up; it was meant more as an announcement than an invitation.

In those days, the Yankees and Dodgers played three exhibition games every spring in New York, either at Yankee Stadium or at Ebbets Field, on the weekend before the start of the season. As it happened, the series that year was on the weekend of our wedding.

Imagine our surprise when our limousine pulled up at Donahue's and, as it did, a bus carrying the whole Yankees team pulled up behind us. We had no idea they were coming. Most of the veteran players, DiMaggio, Page, Henrich, and the rest, joined us at the wedding reception for about 30 or 40 minutes, but Mantle never left the bus. He was too shy. So, Joan and I went onto the bus to shake hands with the handful of players who didn't come into the reception and to thank them for coming. Mantle was one of them.

It was a different Mantle I saw when I rejoined the team in 1953. He was no longer the shy, backward, country boy I had known before. He was more outgoing, more confident, and he was dressing better. The change was miraculous.

What had happened to him was Billy Martin.

While I was away in the army, Martin had nobody to run with, so he somehow settled on Mantle, and the two of them just hit it off from the start. Martin taught Mantle how to dress like a big leaguer, how to order in fancy restaurants, and how to find the hot spots in whatever town they were playing, including New York. Mantle even moved in with Martin at the swanky Hotel St. Moritz on Central Park South.

It was natural when I returned that I would start hanging out with Martin again, which meant we became a trio. I don't know why Mantle and I hit it off so well, but we did. There was nothing about us, or our backgrounds, that was similar or that should have made us compatible. He was a country boy from Oklahoma. I was a street kid from New York. Half the time I couldn't understand what he was saying in that Oklahoma drawl, and he couldn't understand what I was saying in my New York accent. Maybe it was Martin, from Berkeley, California, who bridged the gap between Mantle and me and brought us together.

The three of us were inseparable. Yes, we went out a lot, especially on the road, but I don't want to give the impression it was nothing but party, party, party. We took care of business. I would never go out if I was scheduled to pitch the next day. I'd make sure to get to my room early and get my rest. After I pitched, then I'd join them for a little relaxation.

In New York, while Martin and Mantle would bounce around at the hot spots like 21 and Danny's Hideaway, I would go home to Long Island, to my wife Joan and my kids. Most of the time.

I'm not going to tell you everywhere we went and everything we did, but there's one incident I have to discuss because it was such a big deal at the time. I'm talking about the famous, or infamous, "Copa Incident."

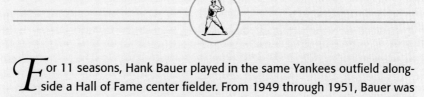

*F*or 11 seasons, Hank Bauer played in the same Yankees outfield alongside a Hall of Fame center fielder. From 1949 through 1951, Bauer was the right fielder (he occasionally played left) next to Joe DiMaggio. From 1952 until he was traded to Kansas City in 1960, Bauer played alongside Mickey Mantle.

Who better, then, to speak about these two Yankees icons?

While Bauer wouldn't get into comparing the two, he did concede that he was closer to Mantle than he was to DiMag. Said Bauer:

> *I didn't spend a lot of time with DiMaggio. By the time I got to the Yankees, he was at the end of his career. Joe was a loner. He wanted to be by himself most of the time, and he wasn't going to spend time with a new guy, anyway.*
>
> *Mickey was different. His first year, three of us shared an apartment over the Stage Delicatessen. It was me and Johnny Hopp and Mick. He was a country boy, very shy at first. That didn't last too long.*
>
> *As players, DiMaggio was a better outfielder. He always got a great jump on the ball and made hard catches look easy. Mickey would outrun the ball. I'm not saying he was better than DiMag, but Mick had*

*more power and he was faster. He stole more bases. He could have stolen a lot more, but those teams didn't run very much. We didn't have to.*

*Mickey struck out a lot, but he was a home-run hitter, and if you look up the records of most home-run hitters, they strike out a hell of a lot. DiMaggio was an exception. He didn't strike out a lot, but when Mick came along, the game started to change, and guys who were home-run hitters were striking out a lot.*

*The things that were similar about DiMaggio and Mantle were that they were both great center fielders, both Hall of Famers, and both were the offensive leaders of our team. I'm fortunate to have played with two greats like that.*

This is what happened as I remember it.

It was in 1957. Martin's birthday was May 16, which happened to be a Sunday. We had a game that day and a day off the next day, so we planned a birthday party. Yogi Berra, Hank Bauer, Gil McDougald, Johnny Kucks, and I went with our wives. Mantle and Martin went stag.

We didn't even plan to go to the Copacabana, a famous nightclub in New York at the time. We had arranged to have dinner at Danny's Hideaway and that would be it. But after dinner it was still early, so Danny Stradella, the owner of Danny's Hideaway, suggested we go to the Copa. He had a table there, and he offered it to us.

It sounded like a good idea, so off we went to the Copa. Sammy Davis Jr. was performing, and we got there in time for his last show.

There was another group seated not far from us at a big, long table. It turned out to be a bowling team, and they had been there for several hours. That was obvious because they were pretty well juiced, and they were making a lot of noise. They started calling Sammy Davis "Sambo" and making other racial remarks.

Bauer yelled over to them and, in a nice way, asked them to cool it. The next thing we knew, one of the guys said, "Who's going to make me?" and got up and came face-to-face with Bauer. Bauer and this guy went off to the back room, and the rest of us tagged along, just in case.

The guy who made the remark to Bauer was the first one in the back room. He got there even before Hank. The next thing I knew, there was a crashing sound, and by the time we got there, this guy is stretched out on the floor. My eyes never left Hank, so I know he didn't do it. To this day, I don't know who slugged the guy. I think it was one of the Copa bouncers, because it was a professional job.

I knew one thing: we had to get out of there fast. If it got into the papers, we'd be in big trouble. Somebody led us out of the Copa through the kitchen, and we all got into our cars and went home.

We tried to keep the whole thing quiet, but somebody tipped off the papers, and the next morning I got a call from Mantle and Martin telling me that George Weiss, our general manager, was fining each of us $1,000.

Eventually, the case went to the grand jury, and we had to hire a lawyer to defend us against charges of assault and disorderly conduct. The grand jury threw out the case. We were innocent, but we never got our $1,000 fine back, and we had to pay for the lawyer, so Martin's birthday party cost us about $2,000 each.

At first, there were stories that Bauer slugged the guy. Then word got around that Martin had done it. Neither of them did, believe me. That guy was lying on the ground before any of us got there.

But Weiss made Martin the scapegoat because he never liked him and was looking for an excuse to get rid of him. The funny thing is that Martin had nothing to do with the fight. He didn't even organize the party; Mantle and I did. It just happened to be Martin's birthday.

Exactly a month to the day after the Copa incident, Martin was traded to Kansas City. It was no coincidence.

Years later, Martin would say, "Weiss got rid of me because he said I was a bad influence on Mickey and Whitey. A bad influence on them? They both made the Hall of Fame and I didn't. Maybe they were a bad influence on me."

With Martin gone, it was just me and Mantle, and we became even closer. On the road, we each had single rooms, but we would arrange to get adjoining rooms, and we'd open the door between the two rooms and turn it into

111

*"DiMaggio and Mantle . . . were both great center fielders, both Hall of Famers, and both were the offensive leaders of our team. I'm fortunate to have played with two greats like that."* —HANK BAUER

Mickey Mantle always maintained that he was better at hitting right-handed than left-handed, but he had more power left-handed.

a little suite. In effect, we were roommates for the remainder of our years together on the Yankees.

Through those years, I came to appreciate Mantle more and more as a player and as a teammate. He was a superstar who never acted like one. He was a humble man who was kind and friendly to all his teammates, even the rawest rookie. He was idolized by all the other players.

I can't tell you how often he amazed me with his exploits on the field, the catches he made, his blinding speed, and, most memorable, his tremendous home runs. He won so many games for me, I've lost count.

I also learned about his remarkable courage. Often he played hurt, his knees aching so much he could hardly walk. But he never complained, and he would somehow manage to drag himself onto the field, ignore the pain, and do something spectacular.

One of the greatest days in my life came when I was elected to the Baseball Hall of Fame in 1974. What made it even more special is that Mantle was elected the same year, and we were inducted together.

The Hall of Fame induction ceremonies in Cooperstown, New York, were on Sunday, August 11, 1974. I was coaching for the Yankees at the time, and we were on the West Coast, but I left after a Friday night game in Anaheim and flew all night to New York. Joan picked me up at the airport, and we drove up to Cooperstown, to the Otesaga Hotel.

My daughter, Sally Ann, and her husband, Steve, came with us, and so did our son Tommy. Our other son, Eddie, was playing for the Red Sox farm team in Niagara Falls, and his plan was to drive over to Cooperstown after playing a game on Saturday night and be there in time for the ceremonies on Sunday.

Mantle had rented a bus, and a lot of my friends and family were invited to ride up on it.

I was nervous on the drive all the way up to Cooperstown, worrying about the speech I was going to have to make.

The best part of the weekend is the private dinner they have on Saturday night just for the commissioner and members of the Hall of Fame. No press, no guests, just the recent inductees and whatever Hall of Famers accept the invitation to come back for the induction ceremonies. It's at this dinner that they present you with your Hall of Fame ring.

Joe DiMaggio was there, and so were Casey Stengel, Hank Greenberg, Satchel Paige, Charlie Gehringer, and Bill Terry. We just sat around telling stories and having dinner, and I had a great time until Commissioner Bowie Kuhn asked me to get up and say a few words. I never expected that, and I wasn't prepared, but somehow I got through it.

After dinner, I went back to my room to work on my speech for the next day. I couldn't believe it when Mantle told me he wasn't even going to prepare a speech.

"You're crazy, Mick," I said. "I'm telling you, you'd better write something down or you're going to be lost for words when you get up there."

Mantle just waved me off and went to play pool with his four sons, Mickey, Danny, David, and Billy, and my son Tommy. They stayed up practically all night shooting pool and drinking beer, and the next day Mantle made his speech off the cuff. He never wrote down a word, and I was nervous for him, but he was sensational.

He had the crowd in stitches. One of the things he talked about was all the bad investments he made, including a chain of Mickey Mantle chicken restaurants. "Our slogan was 'To get a better piece of chicken, you have to be a rooster,'" Mickey said, and it just broke everybody up.

My son Eddie drove all night from Niagara Falls and arrived at 5:00 A.M., but they wouldn't believe he was Eddie Ford, so he wound up sleeping in the lobby.

Steve and Eleanor Clancy, my daughter's in-laws, said they hardly slept all night either, because they had the bad luck to be in the room right next to Casey Stengel, and he kept them up all night talking. The walls were very thin, and they could hear every word he was saying.

Stengel had been up late with us drinking, and he was 84 at the time and a little out of it, so when he got to his room, he was talking nonstop. The Clancys couldn't make out exactly what he was saying, but they said it sounded like he was arguing with an umpire. At first they thought he was talking in his sleep, but then they realized he was wide-awake. Then they wondered who was in the room with him. But they heard only his voice. It turned out Stengel was rooming alone.

I stayed up most of the night trying to write a speech and having a tough time finding the right things to say.

Finally, it was time for the ceremonies. We were all sitting on this veranda outside the library in Cooperstown, the Hall of Famers and the four inductees: umpire Jocko Conlan; "Cool Papa" Bell, an old star from the Negro Leagues; Mantle; and me. Commissioner Kuhn served as the master of ceremonies. He would call each of us up, read what was engraved on our plaque, present us with a facsimile of the plaque, then sit down while each inductee made his speech.

Cool Papa Bell went first, and when it was time for him to speak, he introduced everybody he knew in the audience. He introduced his family, his cousins, his second cousins, his third cousins. He introduced his third-grade teacher. He must have introduced 25 people. But he forgot one. His wife. She was ready to kill him after the ceremonies.

Jocko Conlan was next. He made a nice speech, and then he sat down, right next to me. I hardly was paying attention to him, I was so worried about my own speech. Now it was just 20 seconds before Kuhn was supposed to introduce me, and Jocko grabbed my arm and said, "I'm getting pains in my chest."

"Oh, God," I thought. "The man's going to have a heart attack right here on the stage." I was really shaken up. Jocko was 75 at the time, and I was thinking, "Poor Jocko's going to die right up here." But it turned out it was just the heat and excitement of the day.

When it was my turn, I really didn't make a very good speech. I introduced the members of my family and remembered to include Joan, and I thanked my teammates and the Yankees. Gerald Ford had become president just that week, and I got a laugh when I said, "This is a great week for the Fords."

Obviously, DiMaggio and Mantle stand head and shoulders above all Yankees center fielders. There never will be another like them, but in a short time, **Bernie Williams** has shown that he's a worthy successor to Joe D. and Mantle and deserving of being No. 3 on my list of all-time Yankees center fielders.

In his first 10 years as a Yankee, Williams put up some impressive numbers, numbers that are DiMaggio and Mantle–like. He also had a lot of the same qualities as DiMaggio and Mantle—he has a quiet dignity, he leads the team by example, and he is the heart of the offense. I like Williams a lot. He's a switch-hitter and a good guy, and he puts up great numbers. He would have easily fit on the great Yankees teams I played with.

I don't know much about **Earle Combs**, except that he was the center fielder on the "Murderers' Row" teams of the twenties; he had a career batting average of .325 for 12 seasons, all with the Yankees; he batted .350 in four World Series; he led the league in 1927 with 231 hits, a Yankees record until Don Mattingly had 238 hits in 1984; and he is in the Hall of Fame.

I actually crossed paths with Combs even though he retired 15 years before I got to the Yankees. It happened when I made my Yankees debut in 1950.

Bernie Williams, a switch-hitter like Mickey Mantle, is a worthy successor to Mantle and Joe DiMaggio as the center fielder for the Yankees.

We were playing the Red Sox in Fenway Park, and I came in to relieve Tommy Byrne.

The first three batters I faced got base hits, a single, a single, and a double. Then our first baseman, Tommy Henrich, came to the mound.

"Hey, Eddie," he said, "that first-base coach knows everything you're throwing. He's calling every pitch."

I couldn't believe it because I had thrown only about six pitches, but it was true. When I was going to throw a fastball, the first-base coach would yell,

"Be ready." When I was going to throw a curve, he yelled, "Make him get it up."

The first-base coach was Earle Combs.

**Mickey Rivers** is No. 5 on my list of all-time Yankees center fielders. "Mick the Quick" played only three and a half seasons for the Yankees, but he made his mark. He was the leadoff batter and catalyst for those great teams in the late seventies. In his three full seasons, the Yankees won three American League pennants and two World Series championships.

Mickey Rivers was a Yankee for only three and a half seasons, but in that time he was an exciting and productive player, the leadoff man and catalyst for the team that won three straight American League pennants in 1976, 1977, and 1978.

# Statistical Summaries

## HITTING

All statistics are for player's Yankees career only.

**G** = Games

**H** = Hits

**HR** = Home runs

**RBI** = Runs batted in

**SB** = Stolen bases

**BA** = Batting average

| Center Fielder | Years | G | H | HR | RBI | SB | BA |
|---|---|---|---|---|---|---|---|
| Joe DiMaggio<br><br>*56-game hitting streak is 23 games more than next closest Yankee (Hal Chase, 33 games, 1907)* | 1936–42<br>1946–51 | 1,736 | 2,214 | 361 | 1,537 | 30 | .325 |
| Mickey Mantle<br><br>*Hit most home runs at Yankee Stadium (266), seven more than Babe Ruth* | 1951–68 | 2,401 | 2,415 | 536 | 1,509 | 153 | .298 |
| Bernie Williams<br><br>*Did not commit an error during the 2000 season* | 1999–2000 | 1,237 | 1,463 | 181 | 802 | 119 | .304 |

| (continued) | Years | G | H | HR | RBI | SB | BA |
|---|---|---|---|---|---|---|---|
| Earle Combs<br><br>*First Yankee to lead the league in hits (231 in 1927)* | 1924–35 | 1,454 | 1,866 | 58 | 629 | 96 | .325 |
| Mickey Rivers<br><br>*Hit into only 44 double plays in 5,621 career at-bats* | 1976–79 | 490 | 598 | 34 | 209 | 93 | .299 |

# FIELDING

Statistics are for player's entire career.

**PO** = Put-outs

**A** = Assists

**E** = Errors

**DP** = Double plays

**TC/G** = Total chances divided by games played

**FA** = Fielding average

| Center Fielder | PO | A | E | DP | TC/G | FA |
|---|---|---|---|---|---|---|
| Joe DiMaggio | 4,529 | 153 | 105 | 30 | 2.8 | .978 |
| Mickey Mantle | 6,734 | 290 | 107 | 201 | 3.1 | .985 |
| Bernie Williams | 3,127 | 48 | 36 | 12 | 2.6 | .986 |
| Earle Combs | 3,449 | 69 | 95 | 23 | 2.6 | .974 |
| Mickey Rivers | 3,149 | 95 | 61 | 21 | 2.4 | .982 |

EIGHT

# Right Fielder

I STARTED GAME 1 OF THE 1961 WORLD SERIES and shut out the Cincinnati Reds, 2–0, on two hits. It was my third straight World Series shutout. In the 1960 World Series, I shut out the Pittsburgh Pirates in Game 3 and Game 6. That gave me 27 consecutive scoreless innings in the World Series, and I read in the newspapers that I was closing in on a World Series record for consecutive scoreless innings.

My next World Series start was in Game 4 of the 1961 Series. I shut out the Reds for five innings, but I had sustained a foot injury, and it was hurting me so bad, I had to leave the game.

Jim Coates relieved me and completed the shutout for a 7–0 victory. After the game, some writers came and congratulated me for setting a World Series record with 32 consecutive scoreless innings, and what they told me really shocked me.

1. BABE RUTH

2. REGGIE JACKSON

3. ROGER MARIS

4. PAUL O'NEILL

5. TOMMY HENRICH

They said the record of 29⅔ scoreless innings had been held since 1918 by **Babe Ruth**. I was stunned. I knew Ruth had been a pitcher and that he was converted to the outfield because of his ability as a hitter, but I never realized he was that good a pitcher.

Out of curiosity, I went to the *Baseball Encyclopedia* to look up Ruth's record as a pitcher. What I discovered really opened my eyes.

Ruth had been purchased as a pitcher by the Boston Red Sox from the Baltimore Orioles in 1914, when he was 19. That year, he started 3 games, won 2 and lost 1. The following year, he was 18–8 with 16 complete games, and he followed that up with a big year in 1916. Ruth was 23–12 with an earned run average of 1.75, tops in the American League. He started 41 games and completed 23, had 170 strikeouts in 323⅔ innings, and led the league with nine shutouts.

In Game 2 of the 1916 World Series between the Red Sox and the Brooklyn Dodgers, Ruth gave up a run in the first, then pitched 13 scoreless innings, and the Red Sox won the game, 2–1, with a run in the bottom of the fourteenth.

Ruth was 24–13 with a 2.01 ERA, a league-leading 35 complete games, and six shutouts in 1917, but the Red Sox didn't make it back to the World Series until 1918. Against the Chicago Cubs, Ruth pitched a 1–0 shutout in Game 1, then took a shutout into the eighth inning of Game 4. The Cubs broke Ruth's consecutive scoreless inning streak with two runs in the eighth to tie the score, 2–2. But the Red Sox won the game, 3–2, and went on to win the Series, their last World Series championship.

After the 1918 season, Ruth had won 80 games and lost only 41, and he had pitched 17 shutouts in a little more than four seasons. He was only 23 years old, and he was already considered the best left-handed pitcher in baseball. It's very likely that if he had continued pitching, Ruth would have been regarded as the greatest left-handed pitcher of all time.

But by then, Ruth had begun to show his ability as a hitter. He batted .315 in 1915 and hit four home runs as a pitcher when the league leader, Braggo Roth, hit only seven. The Red Sox realized they had something in Babe Ruth that no other team had, and in 1918 they began to use him in the outfield on days when he wasn't pitching.

In 1918, when the manager of the Red Sox was Ed Barrow, who would later become general manager of the Yankees and assemble those great Yankees teams of the twenties, Ruth pitched in only 20 games and won 13. He played 59 games in the outfield and 13 at first base and belted 11 home runs, tied for the league lead with Tilly Walker.

The mighty Bambino, Babe Ruth, didn't always have a big belly, but he always had those skinny legs. *Photo courtesy of the Baseball Hall of Fame.*

By 1919, Ruth was almost a full-time outfielder. He pitched in 17 games and won 9, but he excelled as a hitter, batting .322 with 114 RBIs and the unheard of total of 29 home runs, the most in baseball history, 19 more than the runner-up in the American League, and 17 more than the National League leader.

When Ruth was sold to the Yankees in 1920, his pitching days were just about over. Mostly as a lark, or for old-time's sake, or just to humor the Babe and give the fans a thrill, he would pitch in five games in his years with the Yankees, and his record was 5–0. But by then he was setting standards as a home-run hitter that were so incredible and never-before-seen as to be mind-boggling.

He kept raising the bar for future sluggers to shoot at. After his 29 homers in 1919, he hit 54 in 1920, 59 in 1921, and then the fabled 60 in 1927. They can talk all they want about Hank Aaron's all-time home-run record, about Roger Maris' 61 in 1961, or Mark McGwire's 70 in 1998, but Babe Ruth remains, and always will be, baseball's all-time home-run king. The "Sultan of Swat."

In a later chapter, I say I believe the greatest change in baseball from my day to today is the emergence of the relief pitcher. The second biggest change has been the home-run explosion.

There are many reasons why major leaguers are hitting home runs in record numbers these days. There are inferior pitching, smaller ballparks, the shrinking strike zone, and the fact that hitters are bigger and stronger than ever. They lift weights not only during the off-season but also before and after games. In my day, lifting weights was frowned upon. They use thin-handled bats to get better bat speed, and they don't care if they strike out 100, 150 times a year, even more. And maybe the ball is juiced.

Whatever the reason, or reasons, baseballs are flying out of ballparks at an alarming rate, and there doesn't seem to be any end in sight. Even "little" guys, 160, 170 pounds, are home-run threats these days.

In the year 2000, 16 major leaguers hit 40 or more home runs for the season. In the early days, it was rare for an entire team to hit 40 home runs in a season. No player hit 40 until Babe Ruth hit his 54 in 1920.

In 1930, only four players hit 40 or more homers. In 1940, there were two. In 1950, just one. In 1960, three. In 1970, six. In 1980, three. And in 1990, two.

*D*id he point?

The controversy, and the mystery, has raged for 70 years. Did Babe Ruth call his home run in the fifth inning of Game 3 of the 1932 World Series against the Chicago Cubs by pointing to the center-field stands, then hitting Charlie Root's pitch to the spot where he had pointed?

The legend, and the story, far overshadowed the Yankees' four-game sweep, signaling their return to baseball preeminence after a three-year absence.

Bad blood between the Yankees and Cubs spilled over because of what Ruth and other Yankees deemed shabby treatment of their one-time teammate, shortstop Mark Koenig (see Chapter Four, page 64).

A mainstay on championship Yankees teams in 1926, 1927, and 1928, Koenig, an aging veteran, was acquired by the Cubs in August and helped them hold off the Pittsburgh Pirates for the National League pennant by batting .353 and providing steady and reliable defense at shortstop. Despite his contribution, Koenig was voted only a half share of the World Series money by his new teammates. The Yankees, led by Ruth, called the Cubs "cheapskates."

Ruth's charges set off a war of words, with not only the players on both teams firing insults at each other, but fans from both cities joining in.

After winning the first two games in Yankee Stadium, the Yankees went to Chicago, where Ruth was the primary target of taunts and insults from the Cubs players and the predecessors of today's Wrigley Field "Bleacher Bums."

When the Yankees batted in the top of the fifth of Game 3, the score was tied 4–4. With one out, Babe came to the plate. He took Root's first pitch for a strike, and as the jeers rained down on him, Ruth raised a finger and pointed in the vicinity of center field. Root delivered again, and Ruth took it for strike two. The jeers grew louder. Again, Ruth pointed in the vicinity of center field.

On Root's next pitch, Ruth unleashed a mighty swing, and the ball soared toward the center-field seats, in the direction Ruth had pointed. Reporters covering the World Series wrote that Ruth had called his shot by pointing to the place he intended to hit Root's next pitch. Others exploded the myth by alleging that Ruth never called his shot.

Ruth himself perpetuated the myth and deepened the mystery by alternately confirming and denying that he did, indeed, call the home run. His story changed frequently depending on his whim and the makeup of his audience, and he took the mystery with him to his grave.

Frank Crosetti, who joined the Yankees that season and took over Koenig's old shortstop position, is the only remaining Yankee who played in the 1932 World Series. His view of what happened in the fifth inning of Game 3 is emphatic.

Said Crosetti:

*Babe never pointed to the center-field seats. What happened, he took Root's first pitch for a strike, and the guys in the Cubs' dugout started getting on him. So Ruth pointed one finger at Root and said, "That's one." Then Babe took Root's second pitch for strike two, and the Cubs got on him even louder. So Babe raised two fingers and pointed toward Root and said, "That's two." He was telling him, "I've still got one strike left."*

*Then the next pitch, he hit into the center-field seats.*

*The next season, I was sitting next to Babe in the dugout one day, and I asked him about it. And he said, "If the writers want to think I called that home run, let 'em." That meant to me that he really didn't call the shot.*

All of this serves only to emphasize the phenomenon of Babe Ruth.

The true measure of Ruth as a home-run hitter is by how great a margin he outdistanced the competition. When he hit his 54 in 1920, the runner-up in the American League hit 19, the National League leader hit 15, and he hit more home runs than any other entire team in the American League.

Again, in 1927, when he hit 60 home runs, he hit more home runs than any other team in the league.

In case you think that Ruth was just a brute—a big, fat guy who did nothing but hit a home run or strike out—consider that he had a lifetime batting average of .342; once batted .393; led the league in batting in 1924 with a .378

Babe Ruth struck this familiar and awesome pose—watching a ball he hit sail out of the ballpark—60 times in 1927 and 714 times in his illustrious career. *Photo courtesy of the Baseball Hall of Fame.*

average; had 136 career triples; had 123 stolen bases; led the league in walks 11 times, including a record 170 in 1923; and never struck out 100 times in a season.

Unfortunately, I never had the thrill of meeting the Babe, who died two years before I got to the Yankees. The closest I came was in 1944, when I was 16. Ruth came to the Loews Theater on Steinway Street in Astoria to help the war effort. We were in the middle of World War II, and if you brought two pairs of your mother's nylon stockings, which were used for making parachutes, you got into the theater free. You could see the movie and you also could see Babe Ruth. For me, Ruth was the bigger attraction.

I got my mother to give me two pairs of her old nylons, and off I went to the theater. Ruth was there. He came on stage, gave a two-minute speech about patriotism, and that was it. It was the closest I came to meeting him.

I remember the day he died, August 16, 1948. I was pitching for Norfolk at the time. We were playing in Richmond, and in the middle of the game there was an announcement on the public address system that Babe Ruth had died. They stopped the game and everybody rose for a moment of silence for the great man.

Through the years, the Yankees have had many outstanding right fielders. Reggie Jackson, Roger Maris, Tommy Henrich, and a current player, Paul O'Neill, make my list. There also were George Selkirk, Hank Bauer, and Lou Piniella. And even Joe DiMaggio, Mickey Mantle, Charlie Keller, Dave Winfield, and Bobby Murcer played there occasionally. But to compare any of them with Babe Ruth would be unfair.

It's doubtful there ever has been a Yankee who attracted more attention and more controversy than **Reggie Jackson**. He was a Yankee for only five seasons, but they were five exciting, spectacular, and turbulent years, filled with great accomplishments for him and the team and with so much turmoil. He certainly made an impact and left a lot of memories, so much so that in the Hall of Fame his plaque depicts him wearing a Yankees cap.

*"If I played in New York, they'd name a candy bar after me."* —REGGIE JACKSON

Jackson became a free agent after the 1976 season. He had indicated he was interested in playing for the Yankees when he told a group of reporters, "If I played in New York, they'd name a candy bar after me."

"If I played in New York, they'd name a candy bar after me," said Reggie Jackson. He did
. . . and they did.

Reggie Jackson loved the spotlight and the big stage, and he always performed at his best in big games.

That was a reference to the popular belief that the Baby Ruth candy bar was named after Babe Ruth, which it wasn't. But that's what people thought, and Jackson picked up on that.

Despite his announced desire to play for the Yankees, there were other teams throwing money at him, and George Steinbrenner still had to woo Jackson. He hustled Jackson relentlessly, wined and dined him, and eventually persuaded him to sign a five-year contract for $2.96 million.

I remember thinking, and hearing, that it was an obscene amount of money to pay any player. But as it turned out, Steinbrenner had the foresight to realize it was a great investment, maybe the best free-agent signing ever. Jackson put people in the seats and helped the Yankees win two world championships. Steinbrenner got more than his money back. In fact, the way salaries started rising, signing Jackson actually proved to be a bargain.

But it didn't take long for Jackson to dive right into the eye of a hurricane of controversy. In his very first spring with the Yankees, he got himself into trouble with a story in *Sport* magazine when he was quoted as saying, "I'm the straw that stirs the drink. Thurman Munson thinks he can stir it, but he can only stir it bad."

Naturally, that didn't go over very well with Munson and a lot of other veteran Yankees who were very close to Munson and appreciated him as the leader of the team.

Then there was the fight in the dugout in Boston between Jackson and Billy Martin, when Martin accused Jackson of not hustling. I hated to see that for Martin's sake, especially because I realized his battle with Jackson was one he could not win. Eventually, his feud with Jackson cost Martin his job.

Jackson feuded not only with Martin, Munson, and other teammates, but also had a few scrapes with Steinbrenner, so that when Jackson's contract ran out, Steinbrenner was so fed up with Jackson, he let him walk. Later Steinbrenner said that was the biggest mistake he ever made in baseball.

Looking back, I see that Reggie Jackson was one of the most controversial and flamboyant Yankees of them all. He loved the big stage and performed best in big games, which is why they called him "Mr. October." His three home runs in one game in 1977 stands as one of the greatest World Series performances for a Yankee or anybody.

What may be overlooked in all the flair and showmanship is the fact that, despite what Martin believed, Jackson always played hard and always played to win. He never dogged it. And he reached 500 home runs when that was still a big deal.

When it comes to **Roger Maris**, allow me to get a little more personal. For a guy who broke baseball's most cherished record when he hit 61 home runs in 1961, Maris was largely unheralded, completely misunderstood, and greatly unappreciated.

But he wasn't unappreciated by his teammates. We looked at him not as the guy who broke Babe Ruth's record but as a complete ballplayer. He was fast, and he was a great base runner with excellent instincts when it came to taking the extra base. And he was as good as I've seen at breaking up the double play.

Defensively, he was outstanding. Again, his speed helped, and he had a great arm and the knack for always throwing to the right base. When Mantle got hurt in 1963 and missed more than half the season, Maris played center field and was as good as any center fielder in the league.

One play stands out as an example of Maris's ability as a right fielder. It happened in the seventh game of the 1962 World Series in San Francisco. We went into the bottom of the ninth inning leading the Giants 1–0. Matty Alou led off the inning with a bunt single off Ralph Terry, who then struck out Felipe Alou and Chuck Hiller.

Then Willie Mays came to bat, the Giants down to their last out, and we were one out away from another World Series triumph. Mays hit a bullet into the right-field corner. When it left the bat, it looked like it would rattle around in the corner and Matty Alou would certainly score the tying run. But Maris came out of nowhere to cut the ball off before it hit the wall. Almost in one motion, he came up throwing a strike to Bobby Richardson, the cutoff man. Richardson whirled and threw a strike to Ellie Howard at the plate, and Alou stopped at third with the tying run. Any other right fielder, and I'm sure the game would have been tied and we might have lost the Series. With his play, Maris saved the shutout, the game, and the World Series.

Terry then faced Willie McCovey, who hit one nine miles but foul over the right-field fence. Then McCovey hit a laser beam headed for right field, but Richardson was there to make the catch and give us the World Series, which would not have been possible without Maris's great play on Mays's hit.

But Maris will always be remembered for 1961 and his 61 home runs that broke Babe Ruth's record. He and Mantle were neck and neck for most of the season chasing the Babe—the "M&M" boys the newspapers called them. I always thought Mantle could have hit 61 homers, or more, that year, but he missed 10 games and played a lot of others in great pain.

Right in the heat of the home-run race, Mantle came down with the flu. He went to a doctor for a shot, and the guy must have used a dirty needle or something because the next thing you knew Mantle developed a very bad infection in one of his buttocks.

I remember going into the trainer's room when our team physician, Dr. Sidney Gaynor, was examining Mantle's rear end. I took one look at the hole and I said to myself, "Oh my God, he won't be able to play the rest of the year."

But Mantle had more guts and desire than any player I've ever known. He came back to play, but the time he lost cost him any chance to beat Maris. Mantle ended up hitting 54 home runs.

I was hoping both of them would break the record, and I admit I was pulling a little more for Mantle. Nothing against Maris, but I had known Mantle for 11 or 12 years, and we were very close. Of course, the thing about any record is that whoever breaks it deserves it. You can't take anything away from Maris. He broke the record. He deserved it.

I liked Maris as a player when I saw him with Cleveland and Kansas City. He always played hard, and he had a perfect Yankee Stadium left-handed stroke. I never thought we had a chance to get him, but when we did, in a seven-player trade with Kansas City before the 1960 season. I figured he was the one guy we needed, the missing link.

In his first year with us, 1960, he hit 39 homers, one behind Mantle for the league lead, led the league with 112 RBIs, and was named the American League's Most Valuable Player. That was only a sample of what was to come a year later.

Roger Maris got all kinds of undeserved grief—and an asterisk—when he broke Babe Ruth's single-season home-run record by belting 61 in 1961.

I can't remember when I started thinking Maris had a chance to break Ruth's record. When he got to 30 homers after only 75 games, the newspapers began to speculate about him breaking the record, and that's when all the nonsense began.

Some old-timers, like Rogers Hornsby, said Maris wasn't worthy of breaking a record held by the mighty Babe, and then Ford Frick, the Commissioner of Baseball, came up with that silly asterisk. That was the first year of expansion, and the schedule was increased from 154 games to 162. Old-timers kept prodding Frick that it wouldn't be fair if Maris broke Ruth's record with the extra games. That's when Frick made his absurd ruling that, unless Maris broke the record within the 154-game span, his record would be noted with an asterisk.

Maris didn't know what was going on. He was only doing his job, and all of a sudden, he was in the middle of this controversy. I felt for Maris. He was being sniped at by old-time players, criticized by fans, and descended upon by members of the press, hordes of them from all over the country. He was under so much pressure that late in the season, in Baltimore, his hair suddenly started falling out in patches. He visited a doctor who said it was merely a case of nerves.

Just about that time, there were stories that there was a feud between Maris and Mantle because of the home-run race—that they didn't like one another and were jealous of one another. This bothered Maris because nothing was further from the truth. He idolized Mantle, and the two of them were close friends. They even lived together that whole season, sharing an apartment with Bob Cerv, another teammate, in Queens, right near the Van Wyck Expressway.

People would talk about this so-called feud, and Maris and Mantle never bothered to deny it; they'd just leave the ballpark together and go off with Cerv to their apartment. I used to laugh about it, and so did Mantle, but I know those stories disturbed Maris.

He had a tough time that season. He just didn't seem to know how to cope with all the attention. He couldn't understand all the criticism directed at him from some old-time ballplayers and some writers who questioned his worthiness to challenge the great Babe Ruth. There were always so many reporters around asking him the same questions over and over, and I don't think

Maris was prepared for it. He was a country boy from a small town in North Dakota, and he had never been exposed to that sort of attention.

As a result of all that Maris was going through, the other players sympathized with him. We all liked him anyway because he was a terrific guy and such a great player and a good competitor and he always put the team first. We came to respect him even more with all that pressure on him—Mantle more than any of us.

It seemed the more pressure there was on Maris, the closer he and Mantle became. Not that there wasn't a good-natured rivalry between them, a sense of competition. That was only natural. They both wanted to lead the league in home runs, and they both wanted to break Ruth's record. That was normal, and the competition brought out the best in both of them.

Then, when Mantle got hurt and he knew his chances of breaking the record were over, he rooted as hard as anybody for Maris.

**Paul O'Neill** is a throwback to the players of my era—solid, steady, a fierce competitor who not only hates to lose but also hates to swing and miss a pitch. He's been a consistent .300 hitter, a big run producer, and an outstanding defensive right fielder since he came to the Yankees in a trade with the Cincinnati Reds in 1993. And here, I want to pay tribute to my pal, Gene "Stick" Michael, who recommended that the Yankees trade for O'Neill and who has done so much to put together the Yankees championship teams of the nineties.

**Tommy Henrich** was a lifetime .282 hitter who hit 183 home runs in 11 seasons, and he combined with Joe DiMaggio and Charlie Keller to form one of baseball's greatest outfield trios ever. He never hit more than 31 homers in any one season and drove in 100 runs only once, but it seems like he did more than that because he got so many big hits. His nickname, "Old Reliable," tells it all about Henrich.

He is also one of the nicest people you'd ever want to meet, and he's the first big-name, established Yankee who befriended me when I joined the team.

When I arrived at the Soreno Hotel in St. Petersburg for my first spring training in 1950, I was met by a photographer who said he needed a picture

135

More than any other modern Yankee, Paul O'Neill (facing) is a throwback. He plays hard and he plays to win.

of me. He took me outside to the shuffleboard courts, and standing there, with a shuffleboard stick in his hands, was Tommy Henrich. I knew him immediately from seeing his picture in the newspapers. The photographer introduced us and asked Henrich if he would kindly pose for a picture with me. Henrich agreed, and the photographer started snapping away.

Henrich was so friendly, he put me at ease right away and made me feel comfortable. The next day, the picture appeared in a New York paper—me and Henrich standing by the shuffleboard court with Henrich holding the shuffleboard stick. It was the first time I ever had my picture in a New York newspaper and it was a memorable one. I'm standing next to Henrich looking at the camera. It's a full-length shot, and my fly is open.

Another Old-Timers' Day at Yankee Stadium and another chance to visit with former teammates and other old Yankees heroes. That's Tommy Henrich in the middle greeting Phil Rizzuto (No. 10). I'm behind Henrich, to the right.

# Statistical Summaries

## HITTING

All statistics are for player's Yankees career only.

**G** = Games

**H** = Hits

**HR** = Home runs

**RBI** = Runs batted in

**SB** = Stolen bases

**BA** = Batting average

| Right Fielder | Years | G | H | HR | RBI | SB | BA |
|---|---|---|---|---|---|---|---|
| **Babe Ruth**<br>*Hit two or more home runs in a game a record 72 times* | 1920–34 | 2,084 | 2,518 | 659 | 1,970 | 110 | .349 |
| **Reggie Jackson**<br>*Hit more homers away (78) than at Stadium (66) as a Yankee* | 1977–81 | 653 | 661 | 144 | 461 | 41 | .281 |
| **Roger Maris**<br>*Did not hit a grand slam during his 61-home-run season (1961)* | 1960–66 | 850 | 797 | 203 | 547 | 7 | .265 |

| (continued) | Years | G | H | HR | RBI | SB | BA |
|---|---|---|---|---|---|---|---|
| Paul O'Neill<br><br>*His Cincinnati and Yankee teams have won 20 of 23 World Series games* | 1993–2000 | 1,117 | 1,290 | 164 | 788 | 58 | .308 |
| Tommy Henrich<br><br>*Had 10 hits in 1947 World Series vs. Brooklyn* | 1937–42<br>1946–50 | 1,284 | 1,297 | 183 | 795 | 37 | .282 |

# FIELDING

Statistics are for player's entire career.

**PO** = Put-outs

**A** = Assists

**E** = Errors

**DP** = Double plays

**TC/G** = Total chances divided by games played

**FA** = Fielding average

| Right Fielder | PO | A | E | DP | TC/G | FA |
|---|---|---|---|---|---|---|
| Babe Ruth | 4,787 | 569 | 179 | 85 | 2.3 | .968 |
| Reggie Jackson | 4,062 | 133 | 142 | 31 | 1.6 | .967 |
| Roger Maris | 2,649 | 76 | 49 | 15 | 2.0 | .982 |
| Paul O'Neill | 3,704 | 117 | 44 | 35 | 2.1 | .989 |
| Tommy Henrich | 3,518 | 178 | 56 | 205 | 3.1 | .985 |

# NINE

# Right-Handed Pitcher

Nine right-handed pitchers in the Hall of Fame have worn the Yankees pinstripes, including some who wore them for little more than a cup of coffee.

For instance, Dazzy Vance, who won 197 games in the major leagues, was a Yankee for only 8 games in 1915 and 2 games in 1918; Burleigh Grimes, who won 270 major league games, won only 1 as a Yankee; Stan Coveleskie got only 5 of his 215 wins as a Yankee; Gaylord Perry was a Yankee for only 4 of his 314 wins; and Phil Niekro won 318 games in his career, only 32 of them for the Yankees.

Even Catfish Hunter, a 224-game winner, won 161 of them, almost 80 percent, with Kansas City and Oakland.

That leaves Red Ruffing, Waite Hoyt, and Jack Chesbro.

1. Red Ruffing

2. Allie Reynolds

3. Vic Raschi

4. Mel Stottlemyre

5. Waite Hoyt

I'm not going to include Chesbro on my all-time list because he played so long ago, I don't know much about him, and I don't know anybody who ever saw him pitch. But he's an interesting guy.

He began his career in 1899 with Pittsburgh and joined the Yankees in 1903, when they were still called the Highlanders. He was sold to Boston in

1909, which means he never actually was a Yankee (the name was officially changed four years later) and he never wore pinstripes (they first appeared in 1915).

Chesbro won 198 games in his career, 128 of them with New York. The reason I say he's interesting is that in 1904 he won 41 games, which stands as a record that I think it's safe to say will never be broken. He also lost 12. That's 53 decisions. Because he appeared in 55 games (of the team's 151), that means he failed to get a decision in only two of the games in which he appeared.

He also had an earned run average of 1.82 that season, pitched 454.2 innings, made 51 starts, and completed 48 games. I guess there was no such thing as relief pitchers in those days. What this tells me is that pitching has changed a lot through the years.

I look at today's pitchers, who rarely are allowed to complete a game. There are reasons for that, and they have to do with the emergence of the importance of the relief pitcher. I'll get into that in greater detail in the chapter on relievers. But I look at the lack of complete games today and realize it was much different in my day. I made 438 starts in my career and completed 156 of them. But the most complete games I ever had in a season was 18 in 1955 and 1956. In 1961, when I went on a four-day rotation and won 25, I completed only 11 of 39 starts. Things were beginning to change as far as the importance of complete games was concerned. But even 11 complete games would be considered a lot today.

When I first started with the Yankees, I met Spud Chandler, a right-handed pitcher for the Yankees in the thirties and forties. He used to talk about how in his day, pitchers completed what they started. He was 20–4 in 1943, and he completed 20 of his 30 starts. For his career, he completed 109 out of 184 starts, so he thought pitchers of my era were a bunch of wimps. I'm sure if Jack Chesbro were around when Chandler pitched, he would have thought pitchers in Chandler's time were wimps. What I'm saying here is that the philosophy of pitching has changed with each generation.

No. 1 on my list of all-time Yankees right-handers is **Red Ruffing**, a Hall of Famer and a Yankee for 231 of his 273 wins, which makes him the winningest right-hander in Yankees history. (Editor's note: Whitey Ford is No. 1 among all Yankees pitchers with 236 wins.)

My choice as the number one right-handed pitcher in Yankees history is Red Ruffing. He came from the Red Sox in 1930 and won 231 games in 15 seasons with the Yankees. More amazing, he hit 36 home runs, had a career batting average of .269, and was used as a pinch-hitter 228 times in his career. *Photo courtesy of the Baseball Hall of Fame.*

Ruffing started with the Red Sox in 1924 and was traded to the Yankees in 1930, another in the long line of stars the Yankees got from Boston. With the Red Sox, Ruffing lost 25 games in 1928 and 22 in 1929, but things turned around when he came to New York. He was a 20-game winner in four consecutive seasons, from 1936 to 1939, and he completed 335 of the 536 starts he made in his 22-year career.

Ruffing also was a terrific hitter, so good he was used as a pinch-hitter 228 times in his career. He finished with a lifetime batting average of .269 and 36 home runs. As a comparison, I considered myself a decent hitter, and my lifetime batting average was only .173 and I hit only 3 home runs.

Red Ruffing made 23 starts in 1941, completed 13, and won 15. In 1942, he started 24 times, completed 16, and won 14. After two years in military service, he returned in 1945, started 11 games, completed 8, and won 7. Then, in 1946, his final season as a Yankee, Ruffing started 8 games, completed 4, and had a record of 5–1. Said Phil Rizzuto about Ruffing:

> By the time I got there [1941] Ruffing was coming to the end of his career. He was a once-a-week pitcher by then. He would pitch every seven days, but he was still an effective pitcher.
>
> He'd come right over the top, and it was tough for hitters to pick up the ball because we played a lot of day games in those days and they didn't have the black background in center field back then.
>
> Ruffing was such a good hitter, they paid him an extra $1,000 or $2,000 for pinch-hitting.

Ruffing had a career average of .254 as a pinch-hitter, 58 hits in 228 at-bats. He batted over .300 eight times, had a lifetime batting average of .269 with 36 home runs and 273 RBIs in 1,937 at-bats over his 22-year career.

Rizzuto played with another great right-handed pitcher, Spud Chandler. Said Rizzuto:

> *Spud Chandler was another great right-hander I loved playing behind. He threw a screwball and a sinker and got nothing but ground balls. I was in the navy when Chandler had his best year [20–4 with a league-leading ERA of 1.64, 20 complete games, and five shutouts in 1943]. Everybody said it was because all the great players were in the service, but after the war, in 1946, Chandler won 20 games again.*
>
> *The best right-handed pitchers I played behind were Vic Raschi and Allie Reynolds. Both were the type of pitchers who would never give in. Bear down pitchers. They'd curve their own mother.*

Here's what Tommy Henrich had to say about Reynolds:

> *Allie Reynolds did a lot of things to help his ballclub. He was always ready to pitch in the big games, to start or relieve. He would offer to go to the bullpen when he wasn't starting, and Eddie Lopat used to tell him, "Don't do that, it will shorten your career." But Allie didn't care. He just wanted to win.*
>
> *[Spud] Chandler had a great won-lost record for his career [109–43, a winning percentage of .717]. And [Red] Ruffing was not only a great pitcher, he could hit. He used to bat like Rogers Hornsby, and people used to say that he couldn't hit like that. Let me tell you, 90 percent of the players in baseball would give their right arm to hit like Hornsby.*

Just as I can't think of Hank Bauer without also thinking of Gene Woodling, I can't think of **Allie Reynolds** without thinking of Vic Raschi. They were two-thirds of the Yankees starting Big Three, with Eddie Lopat, when I joined the team in 1950, and they were two of the meanest men on the mound and the fiercest competitors I knew.

Raschi won 21 games for three consecutive seasons, 1949, 1950, 1951; Reynolds won 20 games only once, 1952; Raschi also had a slightly better winning percentage with the Yankees (.706 to Reynolds' .686), but I give Reynolds the slight edge because of his World Series record (7–2 to Raschi's 5–3) and because he did double duty as a relief pitcher and was a great one.

Allie Reynolds came to the Yankees from the Cleveland Indians in a trade for Joe Gordon after the 1946 season. He was a Native American from

Oklahoma and, naturally, everyone called him "Chief." And he was a chief in more ways than one. He was the boss. Everybody looked up to Reynolds. We were all afraid of him. I was and Mantle was and I think even Martin was. Reynolds was a fierce competitor. He hated to lose, and if you messed up, he'd look at you like he wanted to kill you. It got to the point that you wanted to do well if only to keep peace with the "Chief."

In my first year, we won the American League pennant, and I had the privilege of starting the clinching game in the 1950 World Series. We won the first three games of the Series against the Philadelphia Phillies, the so-called Whiz Kids. Raschi pitched a shutout in Game 1 and beat Jim Konstanty 1–0. The second game went ten innings. Reynolds and Robin Roberts both pitched all the way and we won, 2–1, when Joe DiMaggio led off the top of the tenth with a home run. Lopat went eight innings in the third game and we won again, 3–2, when Jerry Coleman singled in the winning run in the bottom of the ninth.

In 1947, when the Yankees were looking to trade for a pitcher, they consulted Joe DiMaggio (right). He recommended Allie Reynolds (center) of the Cleveland Indians. I shudder to think how baseball history might have been changed if Reynolds stayed with Cleveland and teamed up with the great Bob Feller (left).

So, we had played three games and our starters had pitched 27 of the 28 innings we played.

Game 4 was in Yankee Stadium, a chance for a sweep in front of our fans, and it was my turn to start. We jumped out with two runs in the first on an error, an RBI single by Yogi Berra, and an RBI double by DiMag. We scored three more in the sixth. Berra homered. Bobby Brown tripled in one run and scored on Hank Bauer's sacrifice fly.

We went into the ninth inning leading 5–0. I had allowed only five hits, and I badly wanted the shutout and the complete game, to match Raschi and Reynolds.

But "Puddin Head" Jones led off the ninth with a single, and I hit Del Ennis with a pitch. I got Dick Sisler on a force out and struck out Granny Hamner. I was one out away. Then I got Andy Seminick to hit a drive to deep left, and I thought the game was over and I had my shutout and my complete game. But Gene Woodling had trouble with the sun and dropped it for an error to score two runs and cut our lead to 5–2.

I couldn't blame Woodling. Left field in Yankee Stadium is tough to play, especially in October when the sun shines brightly and the shadows fall early. A lot of outfielders have had trouble out there at that time of year.

When Mike Goliat followed with a single, that brought the tying run to the plate and Casey Stengel to the mound.

I knew he had Reynolds warming up, but I wanted to finish the game, and I begged Stengel to leave me in. He just looked at me like I was crazy and waved for Reynolds. It was the worst booing I ever heard Stengel take at Yankee Stadium. Half of the people booing were my family and friends. But Stengel made the right move. I was getting tired and the Phillies had Stan Lopata, a right-handed power hitter, coming up as a pinch-hitter.

Stengel wasn't fooling around. He wanted to end it then and there. It was getting dark and the shadows were falling in Yankee Stadium. Usually, the first place the shadows fall is around home plate, which makes it even harder to pick up the ball because it's coming out of the light into the dark. Lopata had no chance. Reynolds just pumped three fastballs past him and that was that. Lopata swung, but I'm not sure he even saw the ball.

That's what made Reynolds so special, his ability to start and come back two days later in relief and throw bullets. In his career, he won 18 games in relief and saved 49 others, all this while taking his regular turn in the starting rotation every fourth day.

In 1951, he won 17 games, saved 7, and pitched two no-hitters. The first was at Cleveland in July. His second no-hitter was in Yankee Stadium in September in the first game of a doubleheader against the Red Sox. With two outs in the ninth, Reynolds had to face Ted Williams for the final out. He got Williams to hit a foul pop between first base and home plate. Berra got under it and dropped it. We thought the "Chief" would choke Yogi to death right there on the field, but instead he just asked for the ball and calmly went back to the mound. On Reynolds' next pitch, Williams hit another foul pop between first and home, almost the exact spot as the first one. This time Berra squeezed it for the final out, and Reynolds had pitched his second no-hitter of the season.

*"The best right-handed pitchers I played behind were Vic Raschi and Allie Reynolds. Both were the type of pitchers who would never give in. Bear down pitchers. They'd curve their own mother."*
—PHIL RIZZUTO

In a way, it's a good thing Reynolds isn't pitching today. The way he could blow hitters away for an inning or two in relief, some manager would certainly have made him a closer, and he never would have had the great career he had as a starter, with the 182 lifetime victories, the .630 winning percentage, and the two no-hitters.

**Vic Raschi** was every bit the competitor Reynolds was, but he was quiet. He rarely had much to say. He would just glare at you if you messed up, like Reynolds, but Reynolds was the meaner of the two. Raschi was well liked by his teammates, but he could be mean when he had to be, especially on the mound, where he was the most consistent right-hander I've ever seen.

Late in the 1964 season, Yogi Berra's first year as manager after Ralph Houk moved up to the general manager's office, we were struggling, trailing the Chicago White Sox by six or seven games for most of the summer. It looked like we would fail to make it to the World Series for the first time since 1959.

We had this kid pitcher at our Triple A farm team in Richmond who was tearing up the International League, a skinny right-handed pitcher from the state of Washington with a strange name, **Mel Stottlemyre**. He was 13–3 with an earned run average of 1.42 when he was called up on July 11.

He turned out to be a lifesaver. He was cool and poised for a kid of 23, and he had this great overhand sinking fastball that he kept low all the time and got hitters to beat into the ground. Stottlemyre stepped right into our start-

This gathering of Yankees heroes at another Old-Timers' Day represents four different decades in the team's history (from left): Catfish Hunter from the seventies, Bobby Richardson from the sixties, Vic Raschi from the forties, and Ryne Duren from the fifties.

ing rotation and was 9–3 with a 2.06 ERA and two shutouts. We wound up finishing one game ahead of the White Sox for the American League pennant, and it's clear that without Stottlemyre, our streak of pennants would have ended.

I was the pitching coach that year, remember, and Stottlemyre followed me in the rotation. If there was a doubleheader, we would pitch on the same day. I always would pitch the second game, so I could watch whoever was pitching the first game. If it happened to be Stottlemyre, I would kid him and

In 1964, when we were struggling to catch the Chicago White Sox, the Yankees dipped down into their minor leagues and brought up a young, skinny right-handed pitcher named Mel Stottlemyre, now the team's pitching coach. Stottlemyre won nine of his twelve decisions. We wouldn't have won the pennant without him.

tell him the reason I was taking the second game was that the other team always pitched their better pitcher in the first game and I was exercising my executive privilege to pitch the second game so that I would get to pitch against the easier pitcher.

One time we had a doubleheader against the Indians, and Stottlemyre pitched the first game against Sam McDowell, the Indians' ace.

"Who have you got?" Stottlemyre asked me.

"I don't know," I said. "Some kid they just brought up from the Pacific Coast League."

"Sure," he said. "I get McDowell and you get some kid just up from the minors."

"That's the privilege of being the pitching coach," I said.

Stottlemyre won his game, 6–2, and the "kid" up from the minors turned out to be Luis Tiant, who beat me, 3–0, and struck out 15.

Our opponents in the 1964 World Series were the St. Louis Cardinals. I started Game 1 in St. Louis and pitched fairly well in the early innings. I went into the sixth leading 4–2, and then came trouble.

Ken Boyer singled. I struck out Bill White, but Mike Shannon hit a two-run homer to tie it, and Tim McCarver followed with a double. After McCarver's double, Ellie Howard threw me the baseball, and when I went to take the ball out of my glove, I didn't have the strength in my left arm to grab the ball. My arm just lost all of its strength, just like that. The first thing that went through my mind was that I was having a heart attack because I always heard that when you're having a heart attack, you get a pain in your left arm.

Only this wasn't a pain; it was a numbness in the arm. It had the same feeling you get if you take a rubber ball and squeeze it until you can't squeeze any more. Your arm gets weak. I had no feeling in mine.

Howard came to the mound and asked me what was wrong.

"Ellie," I said, "if I try to throw this thing, I'm not going to reach you."

I couldn't even throw a warm-up pitch. Howard called for Berra and the trainer, and I told them I just couldn't pitch any more, so they brought in Al Downing.

I went to the dressing room, and they called for the Cardinals' doctor. I think he was convinced I was having a heart attack. Richie Guerin, the old Knickerbocker basketball star and a good friend, was at the game, and when he saw me leave the field, he came into the dressing room. He also thought I was having a heart attack.

It turned out to be a circulatory problem, not a heart attack, but I was finished for the Series. I tried warming up a few days later, but I still had no strength in the arm.

I felt bad. I was the pitching coach, and I had planned to start three games in the Series, but now most of the load was on Mel Stottlemyre, and he was only a rookie.

Stottlemyre did a great job. He beat Bob Gibson in Game 2, 8–3, then came back to face Gibson again in Game 5. When he left for a pinch-hitter in the bottom of the seventh, we were behind, 2–0. We tied it in the bottom of the ninth on a two-out, two-run homer by Tommy Tresh, but Tim McCarver hit a three-run homer in the tenth and we lost 5–2.

With the Series tied three games apiece, Gibson and Stottlemyre matched up again in Game 7, both pitching with just two days' rest. Stottlemyre pitched his heart out, but pitching on short rest, he just didn't have his best stuff. Neither did Gibson, but they beat us, 7–5, and we had lost the World Series for the second straight year.

It would be the last time the Yankees were in the World Series for 12 years. Things just started going downhill after 1964. Although I won 16 games in 1965, my circulatory problem kept bothering me, and I retired after the 1967 season. Mantle retired a year later. Tony Kubek retired after the 1965 season, Bobby Richardson after the 1966 season. Age was beginning to show on us.

Those were lean years for the Yankees starting in 1965. We finished sixth in 1965, tenth in 1966, and ninth in 1967. About the only thing the Yankees had in those years was Mel Stottlemyre, who won 20 games in 1965, 21 in 1968, and 20 in 1969, with bad teams. Stottlemyre would never get to pitch in another World Series. If he had been with the teams I played on, he would have been a 20-game winner several more times and might have been regarded as the greatest right-handed pitcher in Yankees history.

As it is, he won 164 games, fifth on the Yankees' all-time list when he retired. He also was fourth in strikeouts, second in shutouts, eighth in complete games, eighth in ERA, seventh in games played, and third in innings pitched. And all with a team that finished higher than fourth just three times in his 11 years.

No. 5 on my list of all-time Yankees right-handed pitchers is another Hall of Famer, a New York kid just like me. **Waite Hoyt** was born in Brooklyn, and he spent 9½ of his 21 seasons with the Yankees, from 1921 to 1930. In those 9½ seasons, he would get 157 of his 237 wins.

After he left the Yankees, he bounced around to five other teams including the Brooklyn Dodgers and New York Giants. So he played for all three New York teams, pre-Mets, that is.

I don't know how he wound up in Cincinnati, but Hoyt became one of the first baseball players to go into broadcasting. He called Reds games on the radio for more than 40 years and was a legend in Cincinnati.

I found this position the toughest to rate in trying to pick an all-time Yankees team. There were so many great right-handed pitchers who pitched for the Yankees, and I don't want to overlook any of them. Rather than run the risk of omitting anyone, allow me to list the right-handers who won 20 games in a season for the Yankees. In addition to those discussed previously, 20-game-winning right-handed Yankees pitchers included: Jack Powell in 1904; Al Orth in 1906; Russ Ford (no relation) in 1910 and 1911; Bob Shawkey in 1916, 1919, 1920, and 1922; Carl Mays in 1920 and 1921; "Bullet" Joe Bush in 1922; "Sad" Sam Jones in 1923; George Pipgras in 1928; Ernie Bonham in 1943; Spud Chandler in 1943 and 1946; Bob Grim in 1954; Bob Turley in 1958; Ralph Terry in 1962; Jim Bouton in 1963; Catfish Hunter in 1975; Ed Figueroa in 1978; and David Cone in 1998.

# Statistical Summaries

## PITCHING

All statistics are for player's Yankees career only.

**G** = Games

**W** = Games won

**L** = Games lost

**PCT** = Winning percentage

**SHO** = Shutouts

**SO** = Strikeouts

**ERA** = Earned run average

| Right-Handed Pitcher | Years | G | W | L | PCT | SHO | SO | ERA |
|---|---|---|---|---|---|---|---|---|
| Red Ruffing<br>*Started six World Series opening games (5–1 record)* | 1930–42<br>1945–46 | 426 | 231 | 124 | .651 | 42 | 1,526 | 3.47 |
| Allie Reynolds<br>*Pitched in with 41 saves (with 4 more in World Series play)* | 1947–54 | 295 | 131 | 60 | .686 | 27 | 967 | 3.30 |
| Vic Raschi<br>*Star of 1948 All-Star Game with three scoreless innings and key hit)* | 1946–53 | 218 | 120 | 50 | .706 | 24 | 620 | 3.47 |

| (continued) | Years | G | W | L | PCT | SHO | SO | ERA |
|---|---|---|---|---|---|---|---|---|
| Mel Stottlemyre<br><br>*Belted inside-the-park grand slam (July 20, 1965)* | 1964–74 | 360 | 164 | 139 | .541 | 40 | 1,257 | 2.97 |
| Waite Hoyt<br><br>*Pitched three complete games in 1921 World Series loss to Giants* | 1921–30 | 365 | 157 | 98 | .616 | 15 | 713 | 3.48 |

# FIELDING

Statistics are for player's entire career.

**PO** = Put-outs

**A** = Assists

**E** = Errors

**DP** = Double plays

**TC/G** = Total chances divided by games played

**FA** = Fielding average

| Right-Handed Pitcher | PO | A | E | DP | TC/G | FA |
|---|---|---|---|---|---|---|
| Red Ruffing | 152 | 684 | 26 | 51 | 1.4 | .970 |
| Allie Reynolds | 111 | 349 | 32 | 22 | 1.1 | .935 |
| Vic Raschi | 84 | 259 | 8 | 20 | 1.3 | .977 |
| Mel Stottlemyre | 242 | 570 | 26 | 38 | 2.3 | .969 |
| Waite Hoyt | 160 | 840 | 36 | 40 | 1.5 | .965 |

# TEN

# Left-Handed Pitcher

I SIGNED WITH THE YANKEES ON OCTOBER 4, 1946, and went to my first professional spring training camp in Edenton, North Carolina, in 1947. I was assigned to train with the Binghamton club of the Eastern League, although I would start my career at a lower level in Butler, Pennsylvania, in the class C Middle Atlantic League.

The manager of Binghamton at the time was **Lefty Gomez**, the great Yankees pitcher of the thirties and forties. I never actually played for Gomez, but he was in charge of my first spring training so, in effect, he was my first professional manager.

It was Gomez who gave me the name "Whitey." There were so many players in camp, and I guess Gomez had a hard time remembering everybody's name, so he gave us all nicknames. I was "blondie" or "Whitey," for obvious reasons. Eventually, he settled on "Whitey."

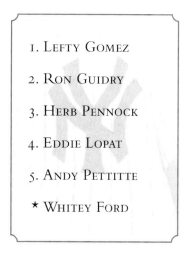

1. LEFTY GOMEZ

2. RON GUIDRY

3. HERB PENNOCK

4. EDDIE LOPAT

5. ANDY PETTITTE

★ WHITEY FORD

It was years before the name stuck. Even after I joined the Yankees, I was still "Eddie." In my early years, I signed autographs "Eddie Ford."

A meeting of the "board of directors" has come to order. That's me in the middle showing my grip to lefty Bud Daley on the far left, lefty "Lefty" Gomez on the right, and a right-hander (how did he get in there?), Art Ditmar, between me and Daley.

It wasn't until guys I had played with in the minor leagues, like Bob Porterfield and Tommy Gorman, joined the Yankees that anybody started calling me "Whitey." They love nicknames in professional sports, and pretty soon all the players were calling me "Whitey." The writers picked it up and started using it in their stories, and that's how the name stuck.

Until she passed away, my mother called me Eddie, and so do others in my family and people who knew me when I was a kid. Everybody else calls me "Whitey." Even my wife, Joan, calls me "Whitey," and we've known each other since we were teenagers.

But getting back to Gomez. I didn't know too much about him back in 1947, except that he had pitched for the Yankees. I had no idea how great a pitcher he was. I also found out later that he hung around with Joe DiMaggio (Gomez was another Yankee from northern California) and that his nickname was "Goofy," because he did some strange things when he was a player. He had a great wit and became a terrific after-dinner speaker. And he also was a practical joker.

I found out about that firsthand.

One of the guys who went to spring training with me was a fellow from my neighborhood, Johnny Simmons. His brother, Connie, was the center for the New York Knickerbockers in the late forties. Johnny also played in the NBA for one season, with the Boston Celtics in 1946–1947, and got to the big leagues for one season with the Washington Senators in 1949.

One night in Edenton, North Carolina, Johnny Simmons and I and another guy, Ray Passapenka, decided to go to the local carnival. We had a 10:00 P.M. curfew, so when it got to be 9:40, we decided we would take one last ride on the Ferris wheel before we went back. We figured it would take five minutes on the ride and that would give us plenty of time to get back to our rooms before curfew.

We got on the Ferris wheel and it went round and round and round. We looked at the clock and it was getting close to 10:00, and we started yelling at the guy running the wheel to stop it and let us off. He pretended not to hear us and we kept going round and round and round. Finally, he let us off exactly at 10:00, and we ran like hell back to our hotel, and who should we run into in the lobby but Lefty Gomez and his wife, the former actress June O'Day.

It was our first spring training, and we were scared. It was five minutes past 10:00, which meant we'd missed curfew by five minutes.

"Where have you been?" Gomez asked.

We tried to tell him about the Ferris wheel and how the guy running it forgot to stop it, but he just looked at us and said, "Bullshit. You're fined $5 each."

About 10 years later, I was with the Yankees, and Joe DiMaggio had a television show between games of a doubleheader. One day, he had his old friend and teammate Lefty Gomez as his guest. I was watching the show on the television set in the players' lounge, and Gomez started telling the story about the Ferris wheel in Edenton.

"I saw Ford get on the Ferris wheel one night," he said, "and I told the guy running the wheel to keep him on until 10:00. I gave the guy a couple of bucks to keep the wheel going, then I walked back to the hotel with my wife and waited in the lobby for my three pigeons to show up."

After the show, Gomez came into the clubhouse with DiMaggio.

"You son of a gun," I shouted at him. "How could you keep that from me for 10 years?"

Gomez started laughing like hell. "I got a lot of mileage out of that story at banquets."

"Oh, yeah," I said. "Well, give me back the $10 you fined me."

So he reached into his pocket, took out a $10 bill, and handed it to me.

I finally got my revenge. He had fined me only $5.

As a pitcher, there was nothing funny about Lefty Gomez. Four times in his career he won 20 or more games, including a league-leading 26 in 1934. He lost only five that season and had a winning percentage of .839, the best in the American League. He also led the league in ERA with 2.33, complete games with 25, innings pitched with 281.2, strikeouts with 158, and shutouts with six. They hadn't started giving out the Cy Young Award yet, but if they had, how could Gomez not have won it?

Gomez finished with a career record of 189–102 and a perfect 6–0 in the World Series. He was elected to the Hall of Fame in 1972, two years before me.

**Ron Guidry** came to the Yankees in 1975. I was their pitching coach at the time. I wish I could tell you that I was the reason "Gator" became one of the greatest pitchers in Yankees history and the American League Cy Young Award winner in 1978, but that wouldn't be the truth.

Guidry came to us from Syracuse late in the season and didn't show signs of any of the greatness he would put on display a couple of years later. He appeared in only 10 games, made just one start, and didn't win a game. In fact, back then there were some who doubted that Guidry ever would make it.

Allie Reynolds (left), Vic Raschi, and Lefty Gomez (right), together won 440 games for the Yankees.

I remember one spring training game in particular for personal reasons. We were playing the Boston Red Sox, and the game was being televised back in New York. George Steinbrenner always wanted to win the televised games in spring training, especially if they were against the Mets or Red Sox. The score was tied 2–2 in the ninth, and Guidry was pitching. The leadoff hitter in the ninth for the Red Sox was Eddie Ford. Yes, my son Eddie. He had signed with the Red Sox out of the University of South Carolina and made it to Triple A. Now he was in spring training, a good fielding shortstop competing for a job with the big club.

So, Eddie leads off the ninth with a single off Guidry, then steals second. With two out, Carl Yastrzemski singles, and Eddie scores what turns out to be the winning run. Steinbrenner went berserk.

*"How the hell can you have this guy Guidry pitching with the game on the line in the ninth inning?!"*
—GEORGE STEINBRENNER

"How the hell can you have this guy Guidry pitching with the game on the line in the ninth inning?!" Steinbrenner shouted. He was ready to ship Guidry out on the spot.

I figured I was in trouble with Steinbrenner because my Eddie had gotten the hit that led to the winning run. Actually, Steinbrenner was very gracious after he had calmed down. "Your boy looked pretty good tonight," he told me.

Guidry did not get shipped out. He stayed with the Yankees for the entire 1977 season and went 16–7. The next year, he had one of the greatest seasons ever for a pitcher.

In 1978, he was 25–3. His .893 winning percentage was the highest in major league history for a pitcher winning 20 games or more. He had an earned run average of 1.74, 16 complete games, and nine shutouts, tying Babe Ruth's American League record set 62 years earlier for the most shutouts in a season by a left-hander.

I thought I had a pretty good year in 1961 when I won 25 and lost 4. As a comparison to Guidry's 25–3 in 1978, my winning percentage was .862, my earned run average 3.21; I had 11 complete games, 209 strikeouts, and three shutouts.

In one game against the California Angels on June 17, Guidry struck out 18 batters, an American League record for most strikeouts by a left-handed pitcher.

For a guy who was only 5′11″ and weighed only 162 pounds, Guidry threw as hard as anybody pound for pound. And he had this nasty, quick-breaking slider that was almost unhittable.

Guidry would be a 20-game winner twice more in his career, 21 in 1983 and 22 in 1985, and he would finish his career with 170 wins and only 91 losses for a winning percentage of .651, which makes me wonder why he has received so little support for the Hall of Fame.

For a skinny guy (5'11", 162 pounds), Ron Guidry "Louisiana Lightning" threw as hard as anybody. I believe his 1978 season, in which he had a 25–3 record, a 1.74 ERA, 16 complete games, 248 strikeouts, and nine shutouts, is the greatest year any Yankees pitcher ever had.

*H*is modesty prevents Whitey Ford from including himself on the all-time Yankees list of left-handed pitchers, so I'll do it for him.

Is there any question that Edward Charles Ford is not only the greatest left-hander but the greatest pitcher in Yankees history?

He is their all-time leader in innings pitched (3,171), wins (236), strike-outs (1,956), and shutouts (45). He's sixth all-time in complete games (156) and fifth in earned run average (2.74). He has baseball's all-time leading winning percentage for pitchers with 200 wins (.690), has the most victories in World Series history (10), and holds the World Series record of 32 consecutive scoreless innings.

Some years ago, when I collaborated with Ford on his autobiography (*Slick: My Life In and Around Baseball*, Morrow), I asked Mickey Mantle to contribute the book's preface for insight into Ford as a pitcher and a man. Mantle's offering follows.

—Phil Pepe

*The Ol' Perfesser, Casey Stengel, used to have a favorite expression that he used when he thought some of his players were getting a little too big for their britches and needed some toning down. He used to call us "whiskey slick." I think Whitey, Billy [Martin], and I heard that expression more than anybody. After a while, Billy and I picked up on it, and we began to call Whitey "Slick," and the name just stuck.*

*The nickname just seemed to fit Whitey perfectly, for so many reasons. He was a city slicker. He was slick on the mound, outsmarting hitters and using every trick in the book and some that aren't. And he liked to have a drink now and again.*

*To this day, I still call Whitey "Slick." And he calls me "Kid." Whitey calls everybody "Kid."*

*It wasn't until after Whitey got out of the army in 1953 that we started hanging around together. The three of us, Whitey, Billy, and me—what an odd trio we were. Me a country kid from Oklahoma. Billy a wise guy from the streets of Berkeley, California. And Whitey, the original city slicker.*

*At first, I didn't know what to make of Whitey. I had never known anybody like him. It was like he was from another world. He always reminded me of James Cagney, the way he strutted around. And the way he spoke! He used to get on me for the way I talked and then I'd go into a bar with him and he would order a "vodker and soder."*

*As a pitcher, Whitey was the best. The Chairman of the Board. I've often said that if I was choosing up sides to pick a team, with every player in the major leagues to choose from, if I had the first pick, I would take Whitey. After all, they say pitching is 90 percent of the game, and there's no pitcher I would rather have on my team.*

*I know I'll get some arguments there from people who say Sandy Koufax was the greatest pitcher of his day or Bob Gibson or Warren Spahn. But Whitey won seven out of every ten decisions, didn't he? And nobody in the history of baseball has ever done that.*

*The amazing thing about Whitey is that he was always the same after a game, win or lose. If I had a bad day, I wouldn't want to talk to anybody. If he lost a tough game, he'd still sit there in front of his locker and answer all the writers' questions. I couldn't do it and I couldn't understand how he could. And it wasn't because he didn't care, because in addition to being the best pitcher I ever saw, he was also the greatest competitor.*

*I remember one game in 1956, either the last game of the season or the next-to-last. Anyway, we were playing the Baltimore Orioles and it was Whitey's last start of the season. He had 19 wins, and he had never won 20 games in his career, and I knew how badly he wanted to win this game. I wanted to win for him just as badly.*

*The Orioles started a young kid named Charlie Beamon, and he beat us, 1–0. The only run scored when I*

Whitey Ford with one of his chief rivals—Sandy Koufax—during the 1963 World Series.

*dropped a fly ball. I wanted to crawl all the way back to Oklahoma. I didn't have the heart to face Whitey after the game, knowing I had cost him a chance to win 20 for the first time in his career.*

*I was almost in tears. I dreaded the thought of facing Whitey. But he made it easy for me. He came up to me in the clubhouse, put his hand on my shoulder, and said, "Forget it, Kid. Let's have a beer!"*

*That's the kind of guy Whitey Ford is.*

*After Billy Martin was traded in 1957, it was just Whitey and me. We used to get adjoining rooms on the road, and we always went out together. We did that until Whitey retired after the 1967 season. I probably have spent more time with Whitey than with any other person on earth. I know Whitey better than I know my own brothers. I've spent more time with Whitey than I have with them.*

*I've known Whitey almost 40 years now, and I never once remember having an argument or a disagreement with him. In fact, I can't*

One of the few times a visit to Yankee Stadium was a sad occasion. This was August 25, 1996, the day they dedicated a plaque to honor Mickey Mantle, who died the year before. To this day I still miss the Mick, who was the brother I never had.

*remember Whitey ever having an argument with anybody. There isn't anybody that I know of who knows him and doesn't like him. That's just the kind of guy he is. He's also the best family man I know. He's totally involved with the lives of each of his three children, and he's devoted to Joan and his mother and Joan's mother and his grand-children. When Whitey's three kids were growing up and we were on the road, he'd always be on the telephone with each of them, staying involved with what was important to them.*

*Don't get me wrong: Whitey can get tough if he has to. But he never has to. He just has a way about him, a way of talking to people that makes them like him.*

*I know men are not supposed to talk about love for other men, especially so-called macho athletes. But I don't mind telling you that I love Whitey Ford. I couldn't love him more if he was my own brother.*

—Mickey Mantle
Dallas, Texas
November 1986

**Herb Pennock**, like so many others, came to the Yankees from the Red Sox in 1923. He pitched for the Yankees for 12 seasons and in his first 5 averaged just under 20 wins a season. He was overshadowed by his teammates Ruth, Gehrig, and the rest, and as a pitcher by his contemporaries Walter Johnson, Grover Cleveland Alexander, Dazzy Vance, and Lefty Grove. But he won 240 games in a 22-year career with three teams and was elected to the Hall of Fame in 1948.

Nobody was more helpful to me when I first joined the Yankees than **Eddie Lopat**. Steady Eddie. He had come to the Yankees in 1948 in a trade with the Chicago White Sox, and he fit in nicely as the left-hander in the Yankees' Big Three of Reynolds, Raschi, and Lopat.

With the Yankees, Lopat won 113 games, including 21 in 1951, and lost only 59, for a winning percentage of .657. In the World Series he was 4–1.

I was in my first Yankees spring training camp only a few days, and I was shagging fly balls in the outfield when Lopat came over and started talking

This group was in place when I joined the Yankees during the 1950 season: catcher Yogi Berra (left), and the Big Three—(from left of Berra) Allie Reynolds, Vic Raschi, and Eddie Lopat. They were saving a place for me.

to me about pitching. We were both named Eddie, we were both from New York City, we were both left-handed, and our pitching styles were kind of similar, so I guess Lopat found in me a kindred spirit. He was ten years older than me, and he had been around the big leagues for seven years, so he probably figured he could be of some help to me. And he was.

I learned a lot from Lopat. In the minors, we never worried much about how to pitch to hitters, but now Lopat was telling me things about pitching.

"You're going to see many of the same hitters year after year," he said. "You're going to have to find out how to get them out. But hitters change and you have to learn to change with them. You might get a guy out with a high fastball one year, but the next year he may start hitting that pitch and you have to switch on him. Move the ball around. High. Low. Inside. Outside.

"You have to get a book on these hitters. How to pitch them. Are they low-ball hitters or high-ball hitters? Who's looking for the curveball all the time? Who's a first-ball hitter?"

Lopat was putting all that in my mind, things I'd never even thought about before. In my three years in the minor leagues I never had anything even resembling a pitching coach. None of my managers had been pitchers. Now I had Jim Turner, who was great with mechanics, and Eddie Lopat helping me learn how to think on the mound. I learned more in one spring than I had in three seasons in the minor leagues, and I owed so much of that to Eddie Lopat.

When I made my major league debut in Boston and got knocked around because I was tipping off my pitches, it was Lopat who worked with me to correct the problem. Lopat and Jim Turner took me on the sidelines the next day and had me go through my sequence of pitches from the stretch position. They spotted the problem in almost no time.

It seems that when I was going to throw a fastball, the inside of my wrist would lie flat against my stomach. But if I was going to throw a curveball, I would set the ball so that the side of my wrist was against my stomach. It was easy for the first-base coach to spot this. But once I knew what I was doing wrong, it was easy to correct it. It was the kind of thing I had been doing in the minor leagues for three years, but nobody ever picked up on it.

That was only one of the little things I got from Eddie Lopat, who was my teammate until he was traded by the Yankees in 1955. But he remained my friend.

**Andy Pettitte**, No. 5 on my list, still has a few more years ahead of him to add to an already impressive record. Pettitte won 20 games for the first time at the age of 24 and had won 100 major league games before his 28th birthday. If he keeps that up, my list of all-time Yankees left-handers may have to be revised in a few years.

# Statistical Summaries

## PITCHING

All statistics are for player's Yankees career only.

**G** = Games

**W** = Games won

**L** = Games lost

**PCT** = Winning percentage

**SHO** = Shutouts

**SO** = Strikeouts

**ERA** = Earned run average

| Left-Handed Pitcher | Years | G | W | L | PCT | SHO | SO | ERA |
|---|---|---|---|---|---|---|---|---|
| Lefty Gomez<br>*Started five of the first six All-Star Games for the American League* | 1930–42 | 367 | 189 | 101 | .652 | 28 | 1,468 | 3.34 |
| Ron Guidry<br>*Won five consecutive Gold Gloves (1982 to 1986)* | 1975–88 | 368 | 170 | 91 | .651 | 26 | 1,778 | 3.29 |
| Herb Pennock<br>*Won clinching game of Yanks' first World Series championship (1923)* | 1923–33 | 346 | 162 | 90 | .643 | 19 | 700 | 3.56 |

| (continued) | Years | G | W | L | PCT | SHO | SO | ERA |
|---|---|---|---|---|---|---|---|---|
| Eddie Lopat<br><br>*Went 2–0 in the 1951 World Series vs. Giants with a 0.50 ERA* | 1948–55 | 217 | 113 | 59 | .657 | 21 | 502 | 3.19 |
| Andy Pettitte<br><br>*Has averaged better than 16 victories and 208 innings per season* | 1995–2000 | 197 | 100 | 55 | 645 | 2 | 834 | 3.99 |
| Whitey Ford<br><br>*Had an ERA below 3.00 in 11 of his 16 seasons* | 1950<br>1953–67 | 498 | 236 | 106 | .690 | 45 | 1,956 | 2.75 |

## FIELDING

Statistics are for player's entire career.

**PO** = Put-outs

**A** = Assists

**E** = Errors

**DP** = Double plays

**TC/G** = Total chances divided by games played

**FA** = Fielding average

| Left-Handed Pitcher | PO | A | E | DP | TC/G | FA |
|---|---|---|---|---|---|---|
| Lefty Gomez | 56 | 393 | 20 | 20 | 1.3 | .957 |
| Ron Guidry | 107 | 307 | 8 | 19 | 1.1 | .981 |
| Herb Pennock | 101 | 834 | 26 | 45 | 1.6 | .973 |
| Eddie Lopat | 100 | 468 | 19 | 30 | 1.7 | .968 |
| Andy Pettitte | 53 | 216 | 12 | 17 | 1.5 | .957 |
| Whitey Ford | 173 | 630 | 33 | 49 | 1.7 | .961 |

## ELEVEN

# Relief Pitcher

I N MY OPINION, THE BIGGEST DIFFERENCE in baseball from my day to today is the emergence of the relief pitcher, the closer or stopper, and how he is used. It's probably the greatest single change throughout the history of baseball.

In the early days of baseball, just before and after the turn of the 20th century, saves were practically nonexistent. Some teams had none for the entire season, and the league's save leader would have two or three.

It wasn't until 1969 that saves became an official major league statistic, but to bring the records up-to-date, statisticians went over every box score from the game's beginning and updated all the records by awarding the saves to the pitchers who earned them.

Back in the early days, teams would have only two, three, or four pitchers, so it stood to reason that pitchers would have to complete games they started. Then they'd take off a day or two and come back and pitch again. There were no relief specialists like there are today. As a result, you will see listed among the yearly saves leaders some of the greatest pitchers of all-time, such as "Iron Man" Joe McGinnity, Chief Bender, Rube Waddell, Christy Mathewson,

1. MARIANO RIVERA

2. GOOSE GOSSAGE

3. SPARKY LYLE

4. DAVE RIGHETTI

5. JOE PAGE

and Ed Walsh. This practice continued into the thirties, when Dizzy Dean and Carl Hubbell are listed among the save leaders.

The first relief specialist of note was Firpo Marberry of the Washington Senators, who achieved the staggering total of 15 saves in 1924. He also started 14 games that year, but he was only 5–7 as a starter. In relief, he won 6 games to go with those 15 saves.

Johnny Murphy of the Yankees was the next prominent relief pitcher. He began his career as a starter and showed promise with a record of 14–10 in his rookie season, 1934. But the Yankees had a good starting rotation in those days, led by Lefty Gomez and Red Ruffing, and manager Joe McCarthy must have figured Murphy would be more valuable coming out of the bullpen than starting. In the five-year period from 1938 through 1942, Murphy led the American League in saves four times, with a high of 19 in 1939.

The relief pitcher began gaining prominence in the forties, when Ace Adams, Joe Page, Hugh Casey, and, later, Jim Konstanty, were used almost exclusively in relief.

In the old days, relievers fell into four categories:

1. starters who would relieve between starts, as Allie Reynolds did so successfully for the Yankees
2. pitchers who were not considered good enough to crack the starting rotation
3. pitchers with a trick pitch (Hoyt Wilhelm's knuckleball, Looey Arroyo's screwball, ElRoy Face's forkball), who didn't have the variety of pitches to be effective for more than a few innings
4. older, veteran pitchers who no longer had the stamina to pitch nine innings

By the late fifties and early sixties, a new breed of relief pitchers had entered the game, pitchers who were used exclusively out of the bullpen, such as Ryne Duren, Lindy McDaniel, Face, Stu Miller, Arroyo, Dick Radatz, Wilhelm, Tug McGraw, and John Hiller.

By the seventies, relievers were attaining superstar status, their value to a team growing dramatically. Relievers like Sparky Lyle, Mike Marshall, Rollie Fingers, and Goose Gossage were considered as important as a team's No. 1 starter. It used to be that pitching staffs were built from the front to the back, with the starters being the No. 1 priority. But times were changing, and some managers were beginning to build their pitching staffs from the back to the front, placing their highest priority on a great closer. Very few teams in the past 20 years or so were able to achieve any success without a great closer.

In the seventies, relievers were still used for more than the inning they are often limited to today. It always seemed logical to me that you bring in your closer when the game is on the line, to get out of a jam in an important game, whether it's the ninth inning, the eighth, the seventh, or earlier.

Take Sparky Lyle as an example. In the 1977 American League Championship Series between the Yankees and the Kansas City Royals, Lyle pitched in four of the five games, for a total of nine and a third innings, and won two of them. In Game 1, he pitched a third of an inning, then came back two days later and pitched two and a third innings. The next day, in Game 4, he pitched five and a third innings for the win, then came back the next day and was the winning pitcher in the clinching Game 5 with an inning and a third.

Two days later, the World Series began against the Los Angeles Dodgers. Lyle pitched three and two-thirds innings in Game 1 and was the winning pitcher. The next day, he pitched an inning in a game won by the Dodgers. The Yankees starter went the distance in three of the last four games, and Lyle wasn't needed. But if he had been, he would have been ready to pitch in any or all four games, and he would have pitched as many innings as he was needed.

In the eighties, the relief pitcher reached his peak in prominence. Relievers like Bruce Sutter, Dan Quisenberry, Dave Righetti, Jeff Reardon, Lee Smith, and Dennis Eckersley were regarded as legitimate superstars of the game and were being paid accordingly.

It was about a dozen years ago that the role of the closer had its most dramatic change, which I attribute to Tony LaRussa, when he managed the Oakland Athletics, and the way he used Eckersley. LaRussa's success caused managers to adopt the same philosophy, which is to bring their closer in to start the ninth inning to protect a lead. He comes in with nobody on and nobody out. It doesn't matter if the starting pitcher has worked eight shutout innings; when the ninth inning comes, out goes the starter and in comes the closer. That's why you have so few complete games today.

It's not Mariano Rivera's fault that relief pitchers are used differently than they were 20 or 30 years ago. He would have dominated in any era. For what he's accomplished in only six seasons, he gets my vote over Goose Gossage, Sparky Lyle, Johnny Murphy, and Dave Righetti as the Yankees' greatest relief pitcher.

Now they have specialists for every occasion. There are long men, who come in if the starter gets knocked out in the first two or three innings; set-up men, who pitch only the sixth, seventh, or eighth innings; pitchers who are brought in to face just one batter—a left-handed pitcher for a left-handed hitter, a right-handed pitcher for a right-handed hitter; and closers, who come in only in the ninth and only with their team leading by one, two, or three runs.

That also explains why relievers pile up so many saves. Through the year 2000, a relief pitcher has saved at least 40 games in a season 56 times, and all but 9 of the 40-save seasons have come since 1990, none before 1983.

Specialization of pitchers has even filtered down to the minor leagues. Pitchers are trained for a particular role in the lowest minors. From their first year as professionals, they are typed as starters, set-up men, or closers and are trained to do that job and that job only. They even have pitch counts limiting the number of pitches a starter can make in a game, which is something that was unheard of in my day.

None of this is the fault of the relievers. This practice is forced upon them by their managers, which is why I'm picking **Mariano Rivera** as the No. 1 relief pitcher on my all-time Yankees team. Rivera has been baseball's most dominant closer over the past five years. It's not his fault that he usually enters a game only in the ninth inning and only when the Yankees are leading by one, two, or three runs. I'm sure if he had his choice, Rivera would prefer to come in earlier, in the seventh or eighth with the game on the line as relievers did 20 and 30 years ago. And I'm just as sure that if he did, Rivera would be just as dominant as he is under the present system.

His career statistics as a Yankee (22 wins and 43 saves in four years) don't justify his making the top five on my list of all-time Yankees relievers, but I wouldn't forgive myself if I didn't make special mention of Luis Enrique Arroyo of Puerto Rico. He had only one great year, but what a year it was. It was 1961, the year I won 25 games, and Arroyo finished most of them.

I had known Arroyo in the minor leagues. He was with Columbus, a St. Louis Cardinals farm team, in 1950 when I was in Kansas City in the American Association. We pitched against one another a few times. He was a short, stocky left-hander, your basic fastball-curveball pitcher, but to be honest, there didn't seem to be anything special about him. He spent six years in the minor leagues before getting to the Cardinals in 1955. But he didn't stick. He was up and down between the minor leagues and the majors like a yo-yo. He was traded to the Pittsburgh Pirates, then to the Cincinnati Reds, and in 1959 he was pitching for the Havana Sugar Kings, a Cincinnati farm team in the International League.

That was just about the time of the Cuban Revolution, and the Reds, fearing for the safety of their ballplayers, moved the team to a temporary home in Jersey City. They played their home games in a big, old ballpark, Roosevelt Stadium, which used to be the home of the old Jersey City Giants of the International League. It was in Roosevelt Stadium that Jackie Robinson played his first game in organized baseball for the Montreal Royals in 1946.

Jersey City is just across the Hudson River from Yankee Stadium, and because it was so close, and they had a team in the league playing in Richmond at the time, the Yankees always had a scout at the games in Jersey City. Arroyo must have impressed one of the scouts because the Yankees bought his contract, and he joined us late in the 1960 season. The scouts thought he could help us as a relief pitcher.

Arroyo won five games in 1960 and saved seven, and because we won the pennant by eight games, you can clearly see what a valuable pickup he was.

In 1961, Arroyo just took command from the start of the season. He became our bullpen stopper. He won 15 games and saved 29, tops in the American League, and he probably got most of those saves in games I started. It got to be a standing joke whenever I pitched. Somebody would ask who was pitching for us, and another guy would say, "Ford and Arroyo."

I really didn't mind. I didn't have to prove to anybody that I could finish what I started. I had led the American League in complete games in 1955 with 18. I was more interested in winning games than finishing them. Arroyo was having such a great year, I was glad to turn my game over to him in the eighth or ninth inning and conserve my energy for my next start. Besides, Arroyo was such a great guy, and he had struggled so long in the minor leagues, I was thrilled with his success.

I hadn't seen Arroyo pitch since the minor leagues, and when he joined us, I couldn't believe he was the same guy. He had come up with a screwball, and that made him a completely different pitcher. Nobody realized it at the time—in fact, Casey Stengel was the first to say it—but Arroyo had more success against right-handed hitters than he had against left-handed hitters. That's because his best pitch broke down and away from right-handers.

I don't remember teams loading their lineups with left-handed hitters against him, but they would have been better off if they had. His screwball was so great, he embarrassed hitters at times. He'd strike them out and make them look bad, or he'd throw that scroogie and get them to hit easy ground balls to the infield. He was awesome.

After that season, I got an award from the New York Baseball Writers. In my acceptance speech, I said they should have two awards, one in English for me, another in Spanish for Arroyo.

My Nos. 2, 3, and 4 relievers on my all-time Yankees team are **Goose Gossage**, **Sparky Lyle**, and **Dave Righetti**. I placed them in that order, but you could throw their names in a hat, pick them out, and place them in the

When Goose Gossage (right) arrived, the mound belonged to him. Here he's telling the pitcher to "get off my mound," as catcher Rick Cerone looks on rather sheepishly.

order in which they are selected—it would be all right with me. That's how close they were in ability and how great they were as relievers.

*"His mound! He was only there for five minutes. But to Goose, for those five minutes, the mound belonged to him."*
—GRAIG NETTLES

Gossage was mean and tough on the mound, the most intimidating reliever I've ever seen. He would glare at batters, then rear back and throw those 98-mile-per-hour fastballs and the hitter usually would have no chance.

Gossage was a fun guy, but a throwback to Reynolds and Raschi in that he was mean on the mound—even to his own teammates. I've heard stories that if he was in trouble and Graig Nettles came over from third to settle him down, Gossage would just glare at Nettles and yell, "What the blankety-blank are you doing here? Get back to third base where you belong."

Lyle was your basic one-pitch pitcher. All he threw was a slider, and it was a beauty. It was slider, slider, slider, one after another. The hitter always knew it was coming, but he rarely could do anything with it.

Lyle was a fun-loving guy who enjoyed pulling practical jokes on teammates and got a reputation for sitting on whipped cream cakes in the nude. He had the same demeanor whether he won or lost. If he came in and stopped the other team, he'd never get too high. Or if he blew a game, he'd never get too low. There was always tomorrow, which is the perfect temperament for a reliever.

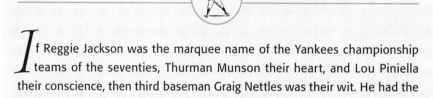

*I*f Reggie Jackson was the marquee name of the Yankees championship teams of the seventies, Thurman Munson their heart, and Lou Piniella their conscience, then third baseman Graig Nettles was their wit. He had the fastest one-liners in the East.

In 1976, relief pitcher Sparky Lyle won 7 games, saved 23, and was voted winner of the Cy Young Award in the American League. The following year,

With his flowing mustache and his vigorous windup and delivery, Goose Gossage was all power and intimidation on the mound.

the Yankees signed free agent Goose Gossage, who soon began to get the "closer" assignments that had belonged to Lyle. Said Nettles, "Sparky went from Cy Young to sayonara."

Gossage, the newcomer, wasn't immune to Nettles' rapier wit. On Opening Day of 1977 in Texas, Gossage made his first appearance as a Yankee in a game-saving situation in the bottom of the ninth. He gave up a home run to Richie Zisk, and the Yankees lost 2–1.

The Yankees won the second day, then lost three straight, one in Texas and two in Milwaukee, where Gossage lost again to the Brewers.

Two weeks into the season, the Yankees went to Toronto and played the Blue Jays on a raw and frigid afternoon. Temperatures were in the forties, but with the windchill factor, it felt like it was below zero.

Players huddled near heaters in the dugout and moved briskly on the field. They played like they couldn't wait for the game to end. With the score tied in the bottom of the ninth, Gossage fielded a ground ball and threw it into right field for an error that allowed the winning run to score. The Yankees had played eleven games and lost six of them, three of the losses charged to Gossage, their $3 million, free-agent relief pitcher.

Not all the Yankees were angry over losing to Toronto on such a cold day, but only Nettles would dare express his feelings. As he left the field and headed for the Yankees clubhouse, Nettles passed Gossage on the mound.

"Thata way to take one for the team, Goose," said the team wit.

Said Nettles:

> I think I was pretty lucky to play with Sparky Lyle and Goose Gossage, two of the greatest relief pitchers of all time. I couldn't choose between them. They were both great. And they weren't very different. They both had the perfect temperament for a relief pitcher: they were the same, win or lose.
>
> If they lost, they'd just shake it off and come back the next time. If they saved a game, they just took it in stride like it wasn't anything special.
>
> There was nothing fancy about them. They just came at you with their best stuff all the time. The big difference between them is Goose threw harder, and he usually came in throwing nothing but fastballs. With Sparky, it was his slider.

*Sparky was one of the first pitchers who was bred to be a reliever in the minor leagues. I remember when he set a record for appearing in the most games without ever making a start. I told him the record should have been appearing in the most games without ever throwing a fastball.*

*They were both great competitors, but Goose showed it more on the mound. The way he would stare down a hitter. He even showed his meanness to me a few times. I'd go to the mound and he'd look at me and he'd start screaming, "Get off my mound."*

*His mound! He was only there for five minutes. But to Goose, for those five minutes, the mound belonged to him.*

Righetti was a rarity for a closer in the eighties. He began as a starter and won 33 games in his first three years. He even pitched a no-hitter in 1983. But when the Yankees needed a closer, Yogi Berra, their manager at the time, asked Righetti if he would give it a shot, and Dave said he would. He went on to be a great closer. In 1986, he recorded 46 saves, which was the major league record at the time and still is the Yankees all-time record for saves.

To give you an idea how the concept of relief pitching has changed, in 1977, when Sparky Lyle had 26 saves and was named winner of the American League Cy Young Award, the Yankees had 52 complete games. The following year, when Goose Gossage led the league with 27 saves, they had 39 complete games.

But in 1986, when Dave Righetti set the major league record with 46 saves, the Yankees had only 13 complete games, and in 1997, when Mariano Rivera saved 43 games, they had only 11 complete games.

What that tells you is that in 1977 and 1978, more pitchers were finishing what they started than they were in 1986 and 1997 and that Lyle and Gossage could have had many more saves if they used relievers then the way they do now.

**Joe Page**, who pitched for the Yankees from 1944 to 1950, is the No. 5 reliever on my list. He may have been the first high-profile relief pitcher in baseball because of his flamboyance.

Sparky Lyle never tried to fool hitters. All he threw was slider, slider, slider. Hitters knew what was coming, but they still couldn't do anything with it.

As a starter, Dave Righetti won 14 games and pitched a no-hitter in 1983. When the Yankees needed a closer, he volunteered for the job and set a Yankees record with 46 saves in 1986.

The call would go to the bullpen in Yankee Stadium, and Page would leap over the short fence in right field that separated the bullpen from the playing field. Then he'd toss his jacket over his shoulder and march to the mound, where he would blow hitters away with pure heat. He led the league in saves with 17 in 1947 (he also won 14 games) and 27 in 1949 (he won 13). And Page's saves were not one-inning outings like you see today.

For example, in the 1947 World Series, he pitched in four games, a total of 13 innings, won one, lost one, and saved one. In the first game, he came in after the starter, Frank "Spec" Shea, was removed for a pinch-hitter in the fifth. Page pitched four innings and got the save. He came back two days later in Game 3, pitched three innings, and was not involved in the decision. Then he pitched an inning in Game 6 and was tagged with the loss, but he came back the next day in Game 7, pitched five innings, and got the win in the game that clinched the World Series championship.

In the 1949 World Series, Page pitched an inning in Game 2, which the Yankees lost to the Brooklyn Dodgers 1–0. He came back the next day and pitched five and two-thirds innings and got the win. Then he came back two days later in the deciding Game 6, pitched two and a third innings in relief of Vic Raschi, and got the save.

Page's last season with the Yankees was my first, 1950, so I didn't get to spend a great deal of time with him. But I did have one memorable experience with him.

It came after we had been in spring training about three or four weeks. We had a game scheduled in Miami. Some of the guys decided to go on a fishing expedition after the game, and I was invited to go along with them. The only fishing I had ever done was by dropping a line into the East River off Steinway Street in Astoria, but I thought this might be fun, a chance to spend some time with a couple of the veteran players on the team and get to know them better. Besides, my hero Joe DiMaggio was going on the trip, and I was excited about spending time with the big guy. I didn't get too many opportunities to hang out with my hero.

There were four of us, DiMag, Page, George Stirnweiss, and me. They had rented a fishing boat that took us out into the Atlantic Ocean.

As soon as we got on board, Page strapped himself into his seat, threw his line in the water, and began trolling. After about an hour, nobody was catching anything, so Page went below to take a nap, leaving his line in the water. That gave Stirnweiss an idea.

He pulled Page's line out of the water and tied a water bucket to it. When a bucket fills up with water, it gets heavy and there's a drag on the line, the same as if a big fish had been hooked. Now Stirnweiss ran down and woke up Page, shouting, "Joe, Joe, get up, you got one! You got a bite."

Page came running up excitely and took his line. The captain steering the ship was in on the gag. Page started reeling in his line, and each time, just as he was about to bring in his "fish," the captain sped up the boat, making it tougher for Page to land his catch. Page would then lose ground, and the line would go out again.

After about a half hour of this, Page was exhausted. Finally, he got his catch close to the boat.

"I got it, I got it!" he shouted.

By this time, all he could see was a big opening in the water, which, of course, was the mouth of the bucket. But Page thought it was the mouth of a fish.

"Look at the mouth on that son of a bitch!" Page shouted. "It's a whopper!"

When he finally pulled it in and saw the bucket, Page knew he had been had. He went ballistic. But he still didn't know who did it, and nobody was taking credit for the prank.

The next day, back in St. Petersburg, we were in the clubhouse and Stirnweiss got a broom handle and a bucket and went running through the clubhouse shouting, "Anybody want to go bucket fishing?"

Now Page knew it was Stirnweiss who had pulled the prank, and Page chased him all over the clubhouse.

# Statistical Summaries

## PITCHING

All statistics are for player's Yankees career only.

**G** = Games

**W** = Games won

**L** = Games lost

**PCT** = Winning percentage

**SV** = Saves

**SO** = Strikeouts

**ERA** = Earned run average

| Relief Pitcher | Years | G | W | L | PCT | SV | SO | ERA |
|---|---|---|---|---|---|---|---|---|
| Mariano Rivera<br>*First to throw final pitch of three consecutive World Series (1998–2000)* | 1995–2000 | 322 | 33 | 17 | .660 | 165 | 395 | 2.63 |
| Goose Gossage<br>*Threw career high 134 innings in 1978* | 1978–83<br>1989 | 319 | 42 | 28 | .600 | 151 | 512 | 2.14 |
| Sparky Lyle<br>*Went 3–0 in 1977 postseason (2–0 in ALCS, 1–0 in World Series)* | 1972–78 | 420 | 57 | 40 | .588 | 141 | 454 | 2.41 |

| (continued) | Years | G | W | L | PCT | SV | SO | ERA |
|---|---|---|---|---|---|---|---|---|
| Dave Righetti<br><br>*Won 29 of his last 30 save opportunities in 46-save season of 1986* | 1979<br>1981–90 | 522 | 74 | 61 | .548 | 224 | 940 | 3.11 |
| Joe Page<br><br>*Picked up a win and a save in both 1947 and 1949 World Series* | 1944–50 | 278 | 57 | 49 | .538 | 76 | 515 | 3.44 |

# FIELDING

Statistics are for player's entire career.

**PO** = Put-outs

**A** = Assists

**E** = Errors

**DP** = Double plays

**TC/G** = Total chances divided by games played

**FA** = Fielding average

| Relief Pitcher | PO | A | E | DP | TC/G | FA |
|---|---|---|---|---|---|---|
| Mariano Rivera | 34 | 48 | 0 | 3 | 0.3 | 1.000 |
| Goose Gossage | 78 | 180 | 21 | 11 | 0.3 | .925 |
| Sparky Lyle | 54 | 198 | 21 | 14 | 0.3 | .923 |
| Dave Righetti | 35 | 150 | 12 | 10 | 0.3 | .939 |
| Joe Page | 17 | 104 | 8 | 4 | 0.5 | .938 |

# TWELVE

# Manager

I N 1949, THE YANKEES SHOCKED THE BASEBALL WORLD when they hired **Charles Dillon "Casey" Stengel** to manage the team. Stengel was 59 years old and believed his major league career was over. He had managed the Oakland club to the Pacific Coast League championship the year before but figured his age would keep him from getting back to the major leagues.

George Weiss, the Yankees general manager, had once hired Stengel to manage in the Yankees farm system. Now he was bringing Stengel in to replace Bucky Harris as manager of the Yankees.

The reason it was such a surprise is that Stengel had failed in two previous shots at managing. With the Brooklyn Dodgers in 1934, 1935, and 1936, he finished sixth, fifth, and seventh. In six seasons as manager of the Boston Braves, his teams finished fifth, then seventh four years in a row, then sixth.

1. CASEY STENGEL

2. JOE McCARTHY

3. JOE TORRE

4. RALPH HOUK/
   BILLY MARTIN

5. MILLER HUGGINS

But with the Yankees, he was an immediate success. He won the World Series in each of his first five seasons, which has never been done before or since. In his twelve seasons with the Yankees, Stengel won 10 pennants and seven World Series championships, the most successful run of any manager in baseball history. That's why he's my No. 1 Yankees manager of all time.

From the first day he saw him in spring training in 1951, Casey Stengel (left) raved about Mickey Mantle's power and speed.

After he was "discharged" by the Yankees following the 1960 season, Stengel, at the age of 72, was the first manager of the New York Mets in 1962. In his first three seasons, the Mets finished 10th all three times and lost 340 games. In 1965, after 91 games, the Mets were 31–64 and last again in the National League when Stengel broke his hip and had to retire for good.

As manager of the Yankees, Stengel was often called a genius. How can a man be such a dummy with Brooklyn and Boston, become a genius with the Yankees at the age of 59, then go back to being a dummy again?

The answer is players. With the Yankees, Stengel had players of championship caliber. But to his credit, he didn't mess things up. He won with those players, and you can never take that away from him. His record as manager of the Yankees may never be equaled.

In Stengel's first season as manager, the Yankees were hit with an unusual number of injuries. Joe DiMaggio, their best player, appeared in only 79 games. George Stirnweiss, their starting second baseman, appeared in only 70 games. Billy Johnson, the third baseman, played in 113 games. There were other injuries, but Stengel managed to cut and paste and patch with what he had. He began his famous platoon system, spotting players against certain teams and certain pitchers. He seemed to push all the right buttons, which earned him the reputation as a genius.

I was pitching for Binghamton in 1949, and I kept an eye on what was going on in New York with their new manager because I thought it wouldn't be long before I was playing for him. I won 16 games for Binghamton, and that gave me 45 wins in my first three seasons in pro ball. I felt I had a good chance to make it up with the Yankees the following year.

It was at that time that I got involved in a small controversy that was none of my doing. We clinched the championship at Binghamton in early September, and the Yankees were in a neck-and-neck struggle with the Red Sox for the American League pennant. A story made the rounds that I called Casey Stengel one day and told him that if he brought me up with the Yankees for the rest of the season, I'd win the pennant for them.

The story was not even close to the truth. What happened was the day after I got home from Binghamton I called Paul Krichell, the scout who signed me, and asked him if there was a chance the Yankees could call me up for the last two weeks of the season. The way I figured it, I was right there in New York, and maybe I could help out by pitching batting practice or being used as a pinch-runner or something.

But I didn't call Stengel. I had a lot of nerve just to call Krichell, but even I wasn't nervy enough to call Stengel directly. I didn't even know him, and I'm sure he didn't know who I was.

Krichell didn't say no immediately. He must have talked it over with George Weiss or somebody, because he called back later and said no. I was disappointed, but looking back, I can see why they wouldn't want some kid from class A hanging around while they were trying to win a pennant.

I met Stengel in the spring of 1950. I had been in training camp about two weeks when he talked to me for the first time—I mean directly to me. I had heard him, of course, in clubhouse meetings.

I had pitched three good innings against the Phillies in Clearwater and had apparently made a good impression on him because he came up to me one day in the lobby of the Soreno Hotel. I was talking to Joe E. Brown, the old movie actor who was doing a postgame television show for the Yankees at the time. Stengel saw us and came over.

"You had a good year down there last year," he said, meaning Binghamton. "I heard you tried to call me and you wanted to get called up last year."

"That was exaggerated," I said.

"Well," he said, "you have a good chance to make this team this year. Just keep your nose clean and do a good job and you really have a good chance."

He never called me by name; he just rambled on about the team needing a fifth starting pitcher and how everybody has an equal chance to make the club and if a young feller bears down and really works hard, he could go north with the team.

Stengel had this unusual way of expressing himself—the writers called it "Stengelese"—saying things without actually saying them, but if you listened closely, you got his message. I didn't think he was goofy. Most of what he said made sense. I always saw him talking to writers. He loved to talk to them, and they loved to listen. He would sit in the bar at the Soreno Hotel, and the writers always knew they could find him there in case they needed to ask him something. I know he stayed up late because every night when I went to my room, if I happened to look in the bar, Stengel was always sitting there, talking to somebody.

Players were never allowed in the hotel bar. That was a rule Stengel had for as long as I played for him. And that went not only for spring training but on the road during the season as well.

"Don't drink in the hotel bar," he used to say, "because that's where I do my drinking."

He didn't want to see what the players were doing, and he didn't want the players to see what he was doing, and I think that makes a lot of sense. I know it avoided a lot of problems.

A few days after Stengel talked to me for the first time, I pitched against the Tigers in Lakeland, and I really took my lumps. My elbow was bothering me at the time, but I wouldn't dare ask out of the game. I pitched and got knocked around, and a few days later I was sent down to Kansas City until I was recalled in June.

When I first came up, Stengel pitched me only against second-division teams. He spotted me against teams he thought I could beat. There were only eight teams in the league then, but he wouldn't pitch me against the first-division teams, Cleveland, Detroit, and Boston. I pitched against the Washington Senators, St. Louis Browns, Philadelphia Athletics, and Chicago White Sox. I wasn't complaining because, by pitching against second-division teams, I won my first seven decisions.

By September, Stengel thought I was ready to step up to better competition. We went to Detroit for a big three-game series, and I was penciled in to pitch the third game. We started the series with a one-game lead over Detroit and lost the first game. But we won the second, and I was matched against the veteran right-hander Dizzy Trout with first place at stake.

After eight innings, we were tied 1–1. Joe DiMaggio hit a home run for us in the sixth or seventh, and they scored their run on back-to-back doubles. I was the first hitter due up in the top of the ninth, and I was sure Casey was going to take me out for a pinch-hitter. But he surprised me and let me hit. I led off the inning with a walk, and we wound up scoring seven runs and winning the game 8–1.

It was a big game for me and for the team. I was over the hump because Stengel trusted me to pitch against a first-division team and I won. The victory kept us in first place, and we never left. We won the pennant by 3 games over Detroit. I started 12 games, finished 7, and had a record of 9–1.

My most embarrassing moment in baseball came in 1954 and involved a decision by Casey Stengel. We were playing in Washington, and President Eisenhower was in attendance. I really wanted to pitch a good game with Ike there. I pitched well to everybody but Jim Lemon, a big, tall, right-handed slugger who hit me like he had stock in me. Lemon got me for three home runs, but each one came with nobody on base.

We went to the bottom of the ninth leading 5–3. I got the first two hitters, then there was a single and Lemon was coming to the plate. And Stengel was coming to the mound. I wanted to finish the game because the president was there, and I begged Stengel.

"Let me stay in, Case," I said. "I'll get him this time."

"What are you, out of your damn mind?" he said. "The guy already hit three home runs off you. You want to try for four?"

Stengel brought in Tom Morgan who got Lemon out, and we won the game. Of course, Stengel made the right decision.

I never complained about being taken out of a game. Naturally, I always wanted to finish what I started, and there were times I figured I should have been allowed to stay in, but I always went along with Stengel's decision. And usually, Stengel was right.

Stengel never showed what he felt. He was just not an emotional man. He never would hug you after a game like Tommy Lasorda did. Casey wouldn't fit in now the way guys hug and kiss one another after a game. His approach was that you were a professional and you were being paid to do a job and you did it. If you didn't do the job, you were gone, so the fact that you were there and he was playing you was compliment enough.

When he came to the mound, he would never talk much about how you pitched. He'd just come out humming, "Do-dee-dum-dee-dum," and he'd never ask you if you were getting tired. He already had his mind made up. Or Jim Turner had told him, "Hey, get him out."

He wouldn't even tell you you were out of the game; he'd just put his hand out, which meant, "Give me the ball," and that's how you knew you were out. And there was no trying to talk him out of it either, as I found out.

One time he came out to get me. He said he was bringing in Johnny Kucks. There were runners on first and third and one out, and we were leading by one run, and he wanted Kucks because Kucks threw a sinkerball, and Casey thought he could get a double play to end the game. He called down to the bullpen and told Darrell Johnson he wanted Kucks, but Johnson thought he said "Trucks." In came Virgil Trucks, and Stengel almost died.

Trucks was in the game, and the first pitch he threw, ground ball, double play, game over. Stengel never admitted to the press the wrong man came in. That's how a manager gets to be a genius.

If you pitched a particularly good game, he might come over and wink at you, but he'd rarely say anything. It wasn't that he didn't appreciate what you did, but he was kind of remote, and it must have been difficult for him to show what he felt.

For instance, he never went out of his way to say "nice game" to you. What he would do, instead, was talk about you to other players or to the writers and make sure you'd hear it. He might say something about you, good or bad, when you were nearby, loud enough for you to hear. He wouldn't mention you by name, but he made sure you always knew he was talking about you.

Even when he took me out of my first World Series game in 1950, he never came to me and said he was sorry he had to take me out. Ralph Houk would have said something like that. Most managers would, but not Casey. It just wasn't his way.

You probably have heard a lot about Stengel's double-talking. It was his greatest weapon whenever the reporters came around, and he would use it perfectly, especially if he didn't want to answer a question. The reporters loved it, and Stengel played the press like a fiddle. They would write about his double-talking, and they helped create his reputation as a character. Everybody won.

But there was never any double-talking in his clubhouse meetings. You always understood every word he said, even if he didn't call you by name. If he had something to say to me and Billy Martin and Mickey Mantle, he would call the whole team together and really chew us out.

"You three," he'd say, looking straight at us. "Don't think you're bullshitting anybody. I know what's going on, and you'd just better stop it, or else."

Then, when the meeting was over, he'd wink at us.

I always thought Martin, Mantle, and I were among Stengel's favorites, but by chewing us out in front of the whole team, what he was doing was showing the younger guys that he would not hesitate to single out a Mickey Mantle, who was a big star, or a Whitey Ford, who was a veteran pitcher. He was using us to make a point with the younger guys, and we understood that.

Stengel would never tell a player he was being sent down. He didn't have the heart. He'd let his coaches give the bad news. After I got banged around in Lakeland that time in my first spring and I was sent to Kansas City, it wasn't Stengel who told me. It was Jim Turner. He said they were sending me down for more experience.

I will say this: everything that Stengel promised me, he delivered. He told Turner to tell me that if I pitched well in Kansas City they'd bring me back, and they did.

The only time I ever got mad at Casey was in the 1960 World Series. I had missed the first six weeks of the season because of a bad shoulder, and, after I returned, I didn't start pitching well until the second half. But I finished strong. I pitched well in my last three or four starts and ended up 12–9. We won the pennant by eight games over the Baltimore Orioles, and I was sure I would pitch the opening game of the World Series against the Pittsburgh Pirates. Casey started Art Ditmar instead and told the writers he was saving me for Game 3 in Yankee Stadium.

That ticked me off. I felt I should have started the first game, which would have permitted me to start three times, if necessary. Stengel's idea was to save me for Yankee Stadium, where left-handed pitchers had an advantage. I never believed in that. It never mattered to me where I pitched. If I had my good stuff, I'd win anywhere. If I didn't have my good stuff, I couldn't win in the Grand Canyon.

Stengel started right-handers in the first two games in Pittsburgh, which we split. I pitched Game 3 and shut them out on four hits. Ralph Terry lost Game 4, and Ditmar got knocked out in the second inning of Game 5, and we went back to Pittsburgh trailing three games to two.

I pitched the sixth game and shut them out again, a seven-hitter. I was pitching as well as I ever had, but I was reduced to nothing more than a spectator for the seventh game, which we lost on Bill Mazeroski's famous home run off Terry in the bottom of the ninth.

Here's Stengel mixing it up at an Old-Timers' Day event.

Three guys named Joe, each a Hall of Famer: that's Joe DiMaggio on the left, and on the right, DiMaggio's first major league manager, Joe McCarthy. The man in the middle is Joe Cronin, who was never a Yankee, but was a Hall of Fame shortstop for the Washington Senators and the Boston Red Sox, and later became president of the American League.

I was mad at Stengel for not starting me in the first game. The way I was pitching, I believed that if I had started three games, I would have won all three and we would have been world champs again.

But Stengel was stubborn. Not only didn't he start me in the first game, he wouldn't bring me back with two days' rest. He never believed in having his pitchers work with short rest.

I was so mad at Stengel, I didn't talk to him on the plane ride back to New York. The funny thing is that a lot of people felt that losing that World Series cost Stengel his job. If we had won the Series, they wouldn't have been able to let him go. So, in the end, it was ironic that his not pitching me three times in the World Series may have cost him his job. It hurt him more than it hurt me, and when I heard that he was let go, I felt bad about being mad at him.

Except for that one time, I thoroughly enjoyed playing for Stengel, and I feel privileged to have played for one of the great managers of all time.

**Joe McCarthy**, Joe Torre, and Miller Huggins are much like Casey Stengel in that they earned reputations as outstanding managers with the Yankees but had little or no success managing other teams.

McCarthy enjoyed a measure of success as manager of the Chicago Cubs from 1926 to 1930, winning one National League pennant and never finishing below fourth. But it was nothing compared with the success he had with the Yankees.

He became manager of the Yankees in 1931 and inherited Lou Gehrig, and he was there when Joe DiMaggio arrived. In 16 seasons with the Yankees, McCarthy won eight American League pennants and seven World Series. His winning percentage of .614 in the regular season and .698 in the World Series are the best in baseball history. With that record you see why he's my pick for No. 2 all-time Yankees manager.

Before he became manager of the Yankees, **Joe Torre** managed 14 seasons with the Mets, Cardinals, and Braves, finished first just once, and lost more games than he won. With the Yankees he inherited Derek Jeter, Mariano Rivera, Paul O'Neill, and Bernie Williams and won four World Series in his first five seasons. If he keeps this up, Torre, my No. 3 pick, could challenge Stengel's record of seven World Series titles in 12 years.

In the winter between the 1960 and 1961 baseball seasons, I went to Madison Square Garden for a college basketball game, St. John's against Kansas. I went because I had ties to St. John's—a lot of friends who went there—and because college basketball was big in those days. The college game had always been more popular in New York than the pros until the Knicks won the NBA championship in the 1969–1970 season. But back in the winter of 1961, the college game was still bigger than the pros, and the St. John's–Kansas game was a "hot ticket."

**Ralph Houk**, who with Billy Martin holds my No. 4 position of all-time Yankees managers, happened to be at the Garden that night. He was living in New Jersey at the time, but he was from Kansas, and he and his wife, Betty, went to the game because of "old school ties," you might say. Houk never attended the University of Kansas, but he knew a lot of people there.

A few weeks earlier, Houk had been named to succeed Casey Stengel as our manager. The Yankees had tried to say that Stengel was stepping down because of his age—he had just turned 70—but the Old Man would have none of it. He kept telling everyone he had been "discharged."

It may be difficult to understand in the context of baseball today, but back then the Yankees considered it an unsuccessful season, and a disgrace, if they did not win the World Series. It had taken the Pirates seven games, and a home run in the bottom of the ninth of the seventh game besides, to beat us in the 1960 Series, and that was a signal to the front office that it was time for a change.

Stengel's age was a factor. A lot of people thought the game had passed him by. Another factor was that Houk had been a coach for the Yankees for three years and was ready to manage in the big leagues. He was only 41, and several clubs had expressed an interest in him as a manager, and the Yankees didn't want to let him get away.

That was fine with me. I liked playing for Stengel, but I liked Houk, too, and I respected his baseball knowledge. We had been teammates on the Yankees in my early years, and even though he never got to play much (only 91 games and 158 at-bats in eight years) because he was behind Yogi Berra, I realized Houk had a good baseball mind. When he wasn't playing, which was often, he would sit in the bullpen or in the dugout near Stengel, observing and soaking up knowledge.

When his playing career ended, Houk used that knowledge to manage successfully in the minor leagues, then he used it as a coach under Stengel. This made Houk a very attractive candidate as a manager, and I was happy our front office recognized that and didn't let him get away. I thought Houk was going to make an excellent manager.

I was even more convinced of that when I ran into him at Madison Square Garden. Houk spotted me and came over to me during halftime.

"I'm glad you're here," he said. "I was going to call you. There's something I want to talk to you about. How would you like to pitch every fourth day this season?"

"Great," I said. I didn't even have to think it over.

Under Stengel, I had pitched every fifth day. I couldn't complain about it, because I was successful. Still, I had never won 20 games in a season because

I never got enough starts. Pitching every fifth day for Stengel, I had won 133 games and lost only 59, but the most starts I ever had in any season was 33 in 1955. I figured if I pitched every fourth day, I would have had 6 or 7 more starts a year, and I would have won 20 a couple of times.

I never liked waiting four days before it was my turn to pitch. I found it boring. I enjoyed pitching. I didn't like watching.

The five-day rotation was actually the idea of Stengel's pitching coach, Jim Turner. He always believed those great pitching staffs the Cleveland Indians had in the fifties—Bob Lemon, Bob Feller, Early Wynn, and Mike Garcia— got tired in the last six weeks of the season. Turner felt you could keep a pitcher fresh by giving him the extra day of rest between starts.

When Houk was named manager, he brought in his own pitching coach, Johnny Sain, who had pitched for the Yankees toward the end of his career. He was still an effective pitcher in his late thirties. He won 25 games for us in 1952 and 1953, then saved 22 games in 1954, at the age of 37.

Sain's theories about pitching were different from Turner's. He believed it was good for a pitcher to throw a lot, even on the sidelines or in the bullpen between starts. He preached that the arm is a muscle, and a muscle gets stronger with use. Unlike a lot of pitching coaches, Sain wasn't too big on pitchers running, but he was big on them throwing a lot.

When he pitched for the Boston Braves, Sain always pitched every fourth day. In six seasons there, he never started fewer than 34 games; he also pitched in relief and never pitched in fewer than 37 games. In 1948, he pitched in 42 games, started 39, completed 28, pitched 314.2 innings, and won 24 games. That year, when the Braves won the pennant, he and Warren Spahn frequently pitched with just two days' rest. The Braves didn't have any other dependable starters, so those two had to carry the load, and that's when they started the slogan, "Spahn and Sain, then pray for rain!"

So it was Johnny Sain who suggested to Houk that we go from a five-man rotation to a four-man rotation in the 1961 season, and I was all for it. I couldn't see any problem with it. I wasn't a hard thrower who relied on 90-mile-an-hour fastballs. I was more of a control pitcher. And I never made a lot of pitches in a game anyway—about 100 to 110 for a nine-inning game. I always believed it was not the number of innings you pitched that took their toll, it was the number of pitches you made.

Going to a four-day rotation turned out to be a great thing for me. In 1961, I made 39 starts, 10 more than the previous season, and had my best year. I won 25 games and lost only 4. It helped that I had Looey Arroyo in the bullpen and that he had his career year with 15 wins and 29 saves.

I completed only 11 games, but I didn't mind because I was happy to be pitching every fourth day, and I knew that was the reason I wasn't going nine innings. If we had had an average relief pitcher, I might have looked at it differently. But we had Arroyo, and I'd always check to see how much he had pitched the days before I started. If Arroyo had pitched two days in a row, I'd try to finish. But if he had a full day's rest, I wouldn't mind him picking me up for an inning or two.

I wasn't looking to bail out of there, but if Houk came to the mound and asked me how I felt, I'd try to be honest with him. If I was tired, I'd tell him, knowing he had Arroyo ready to come in.

For putting me on a four-day rotation and helping me win the Cy Young Award in 1961 and have my only two 20-win seasons (24 in 1963), Houk has a special place with me among managers. He was great with pitchers, which I'm sure was because of his years of experience as a catcher.

Houk had the reputation of being a tough guy, an ex-marine who had earned a battlefield commission in World War II. He was called "the Major." An incident that occurred when he was a coach for the Yankees enhanced his reputation as a tough guy that followed him throughout his career in baseball.

We had clinched the pennant on the road, and we celebrated our victory on the train ride home. One of our pitchers, Ryne Duren, apparently celebrated a little too much and got rambunctious. He spotted Houk smoking a cigar, and Duren went up to him and smashed the cigar in Houk's face. That was a mistake. Houk was livid. He grabbed Duren by the shoulders and was close to decking him. Word of the near fight got out, and from then on there was no messing with "the Major."

Houk never again had to get tough; his reputation took care of that. If we went through a bad streak, Houk would raise his voice at a reporter, and all the players would get the message. They'd say, "Oh, oh, the Major's on the warpath," and the players would just tiptoe around him until he had cooled down.

For me, it was hard to square Houk's reputation as a tough guy with the guy I knew as a teammate. One incident stands out. It's another "fish" story. This also happened one spring training. Houk had a boat, and he loved to fish, especially for saltwater trout. One day he invited me and Gene Woodling to go fishing with him, and we accepted.

I was in the middle of the boat, Woodling in the back, and Houk up front. In the center of the boat was a little pool of water where we would put the fish we caught to keep them fresh.

We were out only a few minutes when we caught three fair-sized trout, which we put in the pool. Houk was all excited because it looked like the fish were biting and we were going to come home with a good catch. Then we went 20 minutes without a bite, and Houk was getting irritable. He was the big fisherman and he was getting nothing.

That gave me an idea. I looked at Woodling and winked, and I whispered for him to give me his line. Houk couldn't see any of this because he was up front and was looking straight ahead, but you could almost see the smoke coming out of his ears.

When Houk wasn't watching I took one of the fish we had already caught, hooked it on Woodling's line, and lowered it back into the water. Now Woodling started fighting like he'd gotten a bite, and Houk heard all the fuss and turned around just in time to see Woodling bringing in another trout.

"Great," Houk said, all excited. "They're starting to bite again."

I took another fish out, put it on my line, and hauled it in. Meanwhile, Houk was going crazy because Woodling and I were landing all the fish and he still hadn't had a bite. You could tell he was frustrated, even embarrassed, because we were catching all the fish and he was getting nothing.

We decided to call it a day, and when we got back to the dock Houk said, "OK, start handing me all those fish."

So we handed him the three fish we had caught early, and that was it, and Houk could see that each fish had about a dozen holes in its mouth where we kept hooking it over and over.

"You son of a bitch," Houk screamed and began chasing us down the dock. I'm sure if he caught us, he would have killed us.

As a manager, Houk was an easy guy to play for. He was a players' manager. He had very few rules. He just let the players play. It helped that he inherited a veteran team—me and Mantle, Roger Maris, Moose Skowron, Tony Kubek, Bobby Richardson, and Clete Boyer—and we policed ourselves.

It may be a stretch to rate Houk among the best Yankees managers of all-time because his career was so short. In his first three years, he won three American League pennants and two World Series, then he was kicked upstairs and became our general manager.

From that point on, the Yankees hit the skids under CBS' ownership and went 12 years without winning a championship. We won the pennant with Berra managing in 1964, then he was fired and Johnny Keane took over and things just got worse. They were so bad, CBS asked Houk to go back down on the field in 1966, but things were not the same. The team continued to lose, and I've often wondered what might have happened if Houk never took the GM job and had stayed on as manager.

As a manager, **Billy Martin** was the remedy for sick teams with anemic records. He was the king of the quick fix who kept his little black bag of tricks packed, a trouble-shooter always ready to move on and provide CPR to ailing franchises. This baseball doctor made house calls.

If Casey Stengel, Miller Huggins, Joe McCarthy, and Joe Torre symbolize managers who floundered with mediocre players and won with good players, Martin, who is tied for No. 4 on my list of all-time Yankees managers, had the ability to win everywhere and with anybody, a fact that is well documented.

In Minnesota he took over a team that had won only 79 games and finished seventh in 1968; they won 97 games in 1969 and finished first.

In Detroit he took a team that had won 79 games and finished fourth in 1970, and he led them to winning 91 games in 1971 and finishing second. Then they finished first in 1972.

In Texas the Rangers had won only 57 games and finished sixth the year before he arrived. In Martin's first full year, 1974, the Rangers won 84 games and finished second.

He moved to the Yankees during the 1975 season with the team's record at 53–51. They would win 83 games that season and finish third. In 1976, Martin's first full season as manager of the Yankees, they won 97 games and their first American League pennant in 12 years.

In Oakland, he took over a team that was 54–108 and finished last in 1979. In 1980, under Martin, Oakland was 83–79 and finished second. In 1981, the A's lost to the Yankees in the League Championship Series.

205

*"When I manage, I have to manage Billy Martin's way. I have to live and die on my own convictions."*

—BILLY MARTIN

In 1987, between his fourth and fifth tenures as manager of the Yankees, Billy Martin made this attempt at explaining Billy Martin:

*My supporters have said I'm one of the best managers in the history of baseball.*

*My critics grudgingly say I may be all right for a year or two, but sooner or later you have to pay the price.*

*What do I think?*

*People talk about the bottom line. All right, let's look at the bottom line.*

*Does Billy Martin win? Yeah, Billy Martin wins.*

*Does he put people in seats? Yeah, he puts people in seats.*

*Does he give all of himself? Yeah, he gives all of himself.*

*I'm the only manager in the history of baseball who took two teams that lost 100 games in one year and won with them the next year. Look it up. In 1973, the Texas Rangers lost 105 games. I got there for the last 23 games. The following year, we finished second in the American League West with a record of 84–76.*

*In 1979, the Oakland A's lost 108 games. The following year we finished second in the American League West with a record of 83–79.*

*What do they want? They want me to manage their way and lose? I can't do that. When I manage, I have to manage Billy Martin's way. I have to live and die on my own convictions. If I have to go down the drain, I've got to be able to say it was my fault. I lost. I can't blame the third-base coach; I can't blame the pitchers; I can't blame the hitters. I can't blame the owner. It was my fault. I didn't win.*

*People are always looking for excuses to justify their decisions. Baseball does that. When I first started managing in Denver, they said: "How can he manage a baseball team when he can't even manage himself?"*

*The next year it was: "He's a hothead. He can't control himself and he can't control his players."*

*Then: "He drinks too much."*

*Every year they try to find something that I do wrong, something to put me down, to discredit me. Something to tarnish my record. But the record speaks for itself.*

*As a manager, I have had my share of Most Valuable Players and a bunch of 20-game winners. Wherever I have gone teams improve and individual performances improve. Do you think that's a coincidence?*

*In Minnesota I had Harmon Killebrew and he won the Most Valuable Player award. I went to Texas and had another MVP, Jeff Burroughs. In fact, in 1974, we swept all the awards—Burroughs, MVP; Mike Hargrove, Rookie of the Year; and I was Manager of the Year.*

*In New York, I had another Most Valuable Player in 1976, Thurman Munson, and another in 1985, Don Mattingly.*

*They say I ruin pitchers. Dave Boswell won 20 games for me in Minnesota in 1969 and never won 20 before or after that.*

*Mickey Lolich and Joe Coleman had their only 20-win seasons for me in Detroit. Lolich won 25 in 1971 and 22 in 1972, Coleman 20 in 1971 and 23 in 1973.*

*Ferguson Jenkins won 25 for me in 1974. The next year I was fired and he won 17.*

*In New York I had 20-game winners Ron Guidry and Ed Figueroa. In Oakland I had another 20-game winner, Mike Norris.*

*Whenever a team is going down the drain and they need somebody to save it, who do they call? Billy Martin, that's who. I've saved two franchises already.*

*I think people should take a look at my record and say, "Look, he did it with five different clubs, not just one like Tommy Lasorda and Earl Weaver. Or like Sparky Anderson, who won with a great team in Cincinnati and a good one in Detroit. Look at the teams he did it with, then measure the man as a manager."*

*That's the true measure of a manager. Not his record alone, but how he improved the teams that others failed with. And how those teams went down the drain after he left.*

*People I've worked for look at how easily, efficiently, and quickly I turned losers into winners and they say, "I can do that." So they fire me thinking they can do the same thing and, of course, they can't.*

Billy Martin, shown here with Reggie Jackson.

*They ask you to lead and to be a manager, then when you try to do it, the owners don't back you. That's the part that makes me mad. They'll say, "Billy, you have to do this, you have to do that, you have to be strict." Then when you're strict, they say you're too strict.*

*Or they say you're too close to the players. Or you're not close enough to the players, you don't communicate with them.*

*How many excuses are there?*

*Whatever suits their convenience at the time they're firing me. They hire you because you're a battler, because you're a competitor, because you're fiery and feisty. They even use these words in their press release announcing you as their new manager: "Fiery Billy Martin, the feisty, etc."*

*Then once they hire you, they try to change you. I don't get it.*

Who knew when they met for a Mayor's Trophy exhibition game in 1981—Billy Martin (left) as manager of the Yankees and Joe Torre as manager of the Mets—that 15 years later, Torre would become manager of the Yankees and exceed even Martin's outstanding record.

But it never lasted. Martin always wore out his welcome, and quickly. He stayed one season in Minnesota, two and a half seasons in Detroit, one and a half in Texas, and three in Oakland. In New York he was fired five times.

This was the burden of Billy Martin. He constantly defied authority. And he seemed bent on self-destruction, unable to control the inner demons that tormented him until his death in 1989.

He tried many times to rationalize his actions, to justify his position, to explain his instability. But how can one explain what he himself does not understand?

In five seasons as manager of the St. Louis Cardinals from 1913 to 1917, **Miller Huggins** finished eighth, third, sixth, seventh, and third. He became manager of the Yankees in 1918 and finished fourth and third in his first two seasons. Then Babe Ruth was obtained in a trade with Boston, and Huggins won six pennants and three World Series championships in the next nine years. That record earns Huggins the No. 5 spot on my list of all-time Yankees managers.

Like Stengel, McCarthy, Torre, and Huggins won championships with the Yankees because they had great players. But also like Stengel, they deserve credit for their handling of those players and getting them to perform up to their ability.

# Statistical Summaries

## MANAGING

All statistics are for manager's Yankees career only.

**G** = Games managed

**W** = Games won

**L** = Games lost

**PCT** = Winning percentage

| Manager | Years | G | W | L | PCT | Pennants | World Series Champs |
|---------|-------|---|---|---|-----|----------|---------------------|
| Casey Stengel<br>*Managed a record 63 World Series games (37–26)* | 1949–60 | 1,851 | 1,149 | 696 | .623 | 10 | 7 |
| Joe McCarthy<br>*Won four straight titles from 1936–39, by 19, 13, 9, and 17 games* | 1931–46 | 2,348 | 1,460 | 867 | .627 | 8 | 7 |
| Joe Torre<br>*Has participated in 0 postseason games as a player, 64 as manager (46–18)* | 1996–2000 | 809 | 487 | 322 | .602 | 4 | 4 |

| (continued) | Years | G | W | L | PCT | Pennants | World Series Champs |
|---|---|---|---|---|---|---|---|
| **Ralph Houk**<br><br>*First former Yankee to lead team to a championship* | 1961–63<br>1966–73 | 1,757 | 944 | 806 | .539 | 3 | 2 |
| **Billy Martin**<br><br>*Had five managerial stints with Yanks* | 1975–78<br>1979, 1983,<br>1985, 1988 | 941 | 556 | 385 | .591 | 2 | 1 |
| **Miller Huggins**<br><br>*First man to have a Yankee Stadium monument in his honor (1932)* | 1918–29 | 1,796 | 1,067 | 719 | .597 | 6 | 3 |

# Index

# S

YOGI BERRA • BILL DICKEY • THURMAN MUNSON
DON MATTINGLY • MOOSE SKOWRON • CHRIS C.
GORDON • BOBBY RICHARDSON • WILLIE RAND
JETER • PHIL RIZZUTO • TONY KUBEK • FRANK CRO
• CLETE BOYER • WADE BOGGS • JOE DUGAN • DAV
WHITE • HANK BAUER • GENE WOODLING • JOE DIM
COMBS • MICKEY RIVERS • BABE RUTH • REGGIE
HENRICH • RED RUFFING • ALLIE REYNOLDS • VIC
GOMEZ • RON GUIDRY • HERB PENNOCK • EDDIE
RIVERA • GOOSE GOSSAGE • SPARKY LYLE • DAVE RI
• RALPH HOUK • BILLY MARTIN • JOE TORRE • MILL
MUNSON • ELSTON HOWARD • JORGE POSADO • L
CHRIS CHAMBLISS • TINO MARTINEZ • TONY LAZZ
RANDOLPH • JERRY COLEMAN • GIL MCDOUGALD •
CROSETTI • MARK KOENIG • GRAIG NETTLES • RED
DAVE WINFIELD • BOB MEUSEL • CHARLIE KELLER •
DIMAGGIO • MICKEY MANTLE • BERNIE WILLIAMS
REGGIE JACKSON • ROGER MARIS • PAUL O'NEILL •
VIC RASCHI • MEL STOTTLEMYRE • WAITE HOYT • L